André Malraux:
Towards the Expression
of Transcendence

More attention has been paid up to now to Malraux's life and thought than to his creativity. To respond to this neglect, David Bevan explores facets as diffuse as Tibetan symbolism, free indirect style, humour, film, death, and oratory in a series of interconnecting essays which, offering a certain unity of discourse in place of any monolithic intelligibility, seek thereby to reflect Malraux's very considerable complexity.

The two principal axes of inquiry are Malraux's ongoing quest for a dimension of transcendence within human life and, at least as compelling, his search for the most appropriate and effective means by which to express a changing awareness of just what that dimension might be.

Not surprisingly, in a world apparently doomed to languish in the spectral shadow of Death, there are certain constants: a yearning for some fraternity to combat man's essential solitude, a refusal to sink without effort into the vortex of the Absurd, a conviction that life is to be lived fully and intensely. The human condition is what it is.

The ways in which Malraux's characters, and of course Malraux himself, cope with this condition reveal a clear evolution, especially from the 1933 novel *La Condition humaine* onwards. The reader follows Malraux from playful adolescence through the dichotomy of anguish and glorification in his middle years, towards the primarily interrogative utterances of the mature man. The often frivolous, sometimes sardonic, humour of youth gives way first to a painful recognition of the abyss, and then to the discovery of a very tentative equilibrium in the philosophy of metamorphosis espoused by an older Malraux. *André Malraux: Towards the Expression of Transcendence* reveals the principal steps by which Malraux achieved that equilibrium.

David Bevan is Professor of French at Acadia University and executive secretary of the Malraux Society.

André Malraux

Towards the Expression of Transcendence

DAVID BEVAN

McGill-Queen's University Press
Kingston and Montreal

© McGill-Queen's University Press 1986
ISBN 0-7735-0552-0

Legal deposit first quarter 1986
Bibliothèque nationale du Québec

Printed in Canada

Canadian Cataloguing in Publication Data

Bevan, David, 1943–
    André Malraux: towards the expression of
    transcendence
    Includes bibliographical references and index.
    ISBN 0-7735-0552-0
    1. Malraux, André, 1901–1976 – Criticism and
    interpretation. I. Title.
    PQ2625.A716Z58 1986   843'.912   c85-099878-6

Contents

Acknowledgments

This book has been published with the help of a grant from the Canadian Federation for the Humanities, using funds provided by the Social Sciences and Humanities Research Council of Canada, and with the help of Acadia University. The author wishes to express his considerable gratitude to both institutions. In addition, a substantial amount of the research involved in the preparation of this study was facilitated by an award from Acadia University's Harvey T. Reid Summer Study Fund.

The author further wishes to thank *Canadian Review of Comparative Literature, Mosaic, Nottingham French Studies, Perspectives in Contemporary Literature*, and *Twentieth Century Literature* for permission to use material which originally appeared in those journals.

André Malraux

Introduction

Le provisoire qu'apporte la
métamorphose rejoint l'aléatoire
qu'apportent les Colloques.
(Malraux, "Néocritique," 307–8)

Le Colloque, en complicité avec
l'aléatoire, semble aux aguets
de la part irrationnelle du
monde ... (ibid., 307)

However self-accusatory an explanation may traditionally be considered, I shall nevertheless begin with one. For it may obviate some
potential admonishment if I admit from the outset that the justification
for the fragmented format of this volume in fact derives in the first
instance from Malraux himself. In the essay "Néocritique" which he
attached to Martine de Courcel's *Malraux: être et dire*, Malraux posited
the emergence of a new literary genre – the colloquium. Such a
development would be the necessary and inevitable corollary of a
modification in our situation in the world, in our perception of time
and space. For earlier generations the classic and consecrated
"study" was "biography" and was characterized by a primarily
affirmative tone that emerged from a heritage embracing a determinist
scheme of History and Evolution. However, the transformation by
which "le biographe change un destin subi en destin dominé"[1] may
well appear as nothing less than fictitious fabrication in a new world
where the fugitive and the tentative are now more readily admitted.
Metamorphosis, argues Malraux, with its accent on the interrogative
and the aleatory, has replaced affirmation as a condition to inform
man's awareness of the nature of his world. Moreover, biography
may well offer little more than the doubtful legacy of a disappearing
individualism, one that is transparently inadequate, in particular, as a
means of approaching the complexity and mystery of creativity and
imagination.

In the light of such proposals it would seem bold, and certainly
ironic, to seek to impose any fixed or monolithic intelligibility on
either Malraux himself or his work. Indeed, Malraux's own funda-

mental preoccupations, certainly from *La Condition humaine* onwards, as Lucien Goldmann has pertinently pointed out, although from an exclusively sociological bias,[2] are essentially pluralist and interrogative. The multiplicity of points of view and exploratory philosophies of that 1933 novel generates, in the wake of the embryonic and prophetic *Noyers de l'Altenburg*, the marvellous riches of *Le Miroir des limbes*. The leaps, juxtapositions, accumulations, and enigmas which determine the modernity of this last text are a formal recognition of the truth of twentieth-century man; and the critic who would approach such an author may do well to seek a similar appropriateness in his vehicle. This is the explanation of Malraux's "colloque": "Sa méthode semble substituer, à l'éclairage calculé, le plus grand nombre d'instantanés, bouts de films, ombres chinoises, etc. ... Ses valeurs ne sont pas celles de la biographie. Un biographe rêve d'épuiser son modèle."[3]

This is also the source, in part, of the present volume. For although it would be naïve or opportunistic to suggest that it responds precisely to Malraux's model, it does attempt to respond to the spirit – a personal, rather than multipersonal, colloquium. There is dialogue between the individual presentations, but it remains multifaceted and unconcerted; the critical scheme of things thus reflects all relationships in our invertebrate world. Malraux is perceived as a shifting, shapeless – beyond mere outline of course – figure characterized more than most by a quality that is proteiform.

Apart from registering changes, only in very focused areas is there any attempt at a "statement"; the strait-jacket of *a*, or even worse *the*, study was deemed to run the risk of either repeating, in whole or in part, the existing accepted overviews of Malraux, or of constraining critical material that was, suitably and unrepentantly, diffuse. For a further variable must be signalled at the more humble level of the critic. Readings of Malraux texts over some two decades bring with them a diverse, perhaps cumulative, often contradictory, experience in the reader. This other multiplicity has again been permitted and encouraged by the retention of interpretations and comments that may well offer some degree of conflict or overlap, and by the acceptance of passages in one chapter that are the stimulus for expansion in another.

Nevertheless, although there is certainly no continuous argument as such, the interconnected spotlights do offer, inevitably, a considerable unity of discourse. In this the two principal axes of inquiry – both in substantive and formal terms – are Malraux's ongoing quest for a dimension of transcendence within human life and, essentially, his attendant search for the most appropriate and effective means by which to express a changing awareness of just what that dimension might be.

I hope, therefore, that the resultant pages will not be misconstrued entirely as a random offering of ill assorted, unconnected, or repetitious notes, but taken as a serious attempt to echo Malraux's own plea in "Néocritique," and to underscore the vital flexibility that must typify creation *and* criticism. Espousing and translating Malraux's own neologism, one might invoke a term such as "neo-criticism," but it would be far less pretentious simply to emphasize that the chosen tone is a recognition in all humility of the utter relativity of any critical sentence. These juxtaposed essays, tentative and interrogative, devoid of any falsifying or presumptuous unity, are therefore no more than a provisional comment.

And yet I would hope that in another decade or so a similar volume might appear – and be no more definitive.

CHAPTER ONE

On "Le Miroir des limbes"

Notre civilisation qui, dans ses sciences
comme dans sa pensée, se fonde sur des
questions, commence à reconnaître une de ses
voix secrètes dans les hautes expressions de
l'interrogation ... de Tolstoï et de Dostoïevski
à Proust, à Joyce et à Faulkner, une des plus
profondes coulées du roman occidental est faite
d'interrogation du destin. (Malraux, "Préface"
to Manès Sperber, *Qu'une larme dans l'océan*,
141)[1]

After some nine years of fragmented publication in individual
volumes, and after a considerable amount of modification of those
earlier versions, the definitive edition of the monumental *Miroir des
limbes* finally appeared in 1976. Critical reception was not entirely
favourable: "Des méditations sibyllines, des divagations pythago-
riciennes, des révélations d'hypothèses enfantines... Que tout cela
est allégorique, ténébreux, confus, démesuré!"[2] Although these
words are in fact taken from a review of Victor Hugo's *Légende des
siècles*, which appeared in *Le Journal des débats* over a century ago,
they were pointedly revived by one reader of Malraux to characterize
public comment on *Le Miroir des limbes*. And yet I should like to
contend that, far from being sibylline or Pythagorean, obscure or
confused, the work in question should rather be acknowledged as
Malraux's most significant statement, a culmination, after a series of
preliminary novelistic exercises that must now be seen as a preparation rather than a fulfilment. Certainly Malraux himself left Jean
Lacouture in no doubt as to the importance he himself attached to
the volume, and the biographer is able to affirm unequivocally in *Le
Magazine littéraire* "le livre auquel Malraux tient le plus, le plus
significatif."[3] Even more specifically, on the occasion of the original
publication of *Antimémoires*, the first section of *Le Miroir des limbes*,
Malraux stressed the crucial existence of an "architecture intérieure
extrêmement forte qu'on ne distinguerait pas très bien au début, mais
qu'on verrait clairement plus tard."[4]

However, before proceeding to establish the principal lines of that
architecture, an informed, semantic glance over some of the titles and
subtitles would already serve to orientate any analysis. In the first

place "Le Miroir des limbes" evokes, before even opening the book, some indirect reflection of an uncertain state between life and eternity – or, within the appropriate vernacular of our particular century, between *être* and *néant*. Thereafter, one could cite the titles of the two basic parts: "Antimémoires" and "La Corde et les souris." The first, by its prefix, refuses both the factual minutiae and the psychoanalytical introspection of the traditional memoirs, implying perhaps a contrasting approach beyond the limitations of mere autobiography. "La Corde et les souris" – the original title was "Métamorphoses," less provocative but more transparent – established the importance of the subsequent exergual parable which teaches, among other things, that art is capable, miraculously, of extending life.

Nor should one ignore those lesser volume titles which were thereafter absorbed into the final work, for those too offer an early indication of the reader's prospective itinerary. For example, "La Tête d'obsidienne" recalls a pre-Columbian relic, a skull carved in stone, an image of Death which, for Malraux, "transcende les civilisations."[5] Or else there is "Lazare," which becomes the final part of *Le Miroir des limbes*, announcing from the title-page a man both dead and alive, beyond the limits of normal existence.

Already, in view of a certain convergence in the above, it should not seem excessively reckless to posit the likelihood of a preoccupation throughout the volume in question with the notion – and therefore the expression – of transcendence. There is no doubt that the principal axes of the narrative can be shown to derive from that very concern. Let us first consider the axis of atemporality, and the associated aspatiality, to which some previous commentators have already made reference.

A continuum of the referential, of the remembered, and of the imaginary brings with it inevitably an accompanying dislocation of external notions of time and space. In a narrative such a condition is likely to arise most frequently because of an author's desire to communicate the totality of a subjectivity. However, in the light of other devices on this occasion and, in particular, because of the continual fragmentation of point of view, it seems more likely that if, by such dislocation in *Le Miroir des limbes*, Malraux aspires to a vehicle which "transcends" conventional modes of expression, it is in order to communicate transcendence itself. It is clear that, in the guise of metempsychosis, this is precisely the focal point of the elephant's meditation in the Buddhist text which Malraux chose to place on the title-page of his work: "L'éléphant est le plus sage de tous les animaux, le seul qui se souvienne de ses vies antérieures, aussi se tient-il longtemps tranquille, méditant à leur sujet."[6]

That meditation heralds a prodigious temporal and spatial accumulation of which the outstanding structural characteristic, rather than any rigorous logic, any chronology, or any causality, is associationism – as a contemporary event in a specific location releases unfailingly some sympathetic recollection, vision, or creative reverie. Thus, for example, do the funeral chambers of the pharaohs alternate with Hitler's dark bunker under Nuremberg stadium, before emerging into the Lascaux caves among the intruding "maquisards."

Elsewhere, it is the enumeration of sundry dates, both at the head of and during the various chapters, that imposes succinctly and yet provocatively a confrontation of different time-periods, inevitably accompanied by an interweaving of diverse places: 1944, 1965, Crete, Paris, the Vercors, Lyon – and the reader is still on the first page! Already the events being described are bathed, as will continue to be the case in the pages which follow, in a kind of cosmic aura: "Nous poursuivions la conversation sans fin de ceux qui se retrouvent dans l'odeur du village nocturne," or else: "Il leva ses bras de bûcheron dans la nuit pleine d'étoiles."[7]

The second structural axis which I should like to recognize, indissociable from the preceding one despite our present critical vivisection, is one which interweaves unremittingly *reality* and *fiction*. Once again the validity of this reading seems to be attested by the author himself, who asserts very early in the volume that: "En face de l'inconnu, certains de nos rêves n'ont pas moins de signification que nos souvenirs."[8] But undoubtedly the key incident is the revelation of the Canton museum. There, a museum, which according to its conventional designation is supposed, scientifically, to represent and reconstruct history, is discovered to be less *true* than a novel, certainly less true than *La Condition humaine*. For this *official* museum has contrived a curious history in which neither the Russians nor Chang-Kai-Chek have ever existed!

At another level few readers could fail to be struck by the extent to which a filiation with Malraux's fictional writings is in evidence. Allusions, the borrowing of novel titles for certain chapters, and long extracts, revive and re-situate the affective force of the works of pure imagination. Moreover, there are passages and quotations too taken from other writers – from a fairy story, a fable, a Greek play, newspapers. On every page this juxtaposition of real and imaginary bears witness to an attempt to forge a new literary expression astride consecrated genres.

Indeed, one can go even further, for there are moments when the frontier between the real world and the imaginary seems to be effaced almost entirely. For instance, the scenario about Mayrena acquires new status as a "second-level" fiction, written apparently by "Clappique," a character already fictional himself; and yet we are obviously dealing with *Le Règne du malin*, a genuine filmscript written by Malraux himself in the early forties. Similarly, the passages presented as interviews, which, had they been taken down stenographically at the time, would have provided very real and authentic documentation, are in fact transfigurations – interviews only therefore "comme *La Condition humaine* était un reportage"[9] – to the point that it is sometimes extremely difficult to be certain just who is speaking.

The single word which once more brings together these twin axes is one which, having virtually disappeared for several centuries, was revived by Malraux in the 1920s. The word, of course, is "farfelu," and its resonance embraces all that is beyond the logical and reasonable; it evokes a level that is mythical and universal: "J'aime les musées farfelus parce qu'ils jouent avec l'éternité,"[10] writes Malraux. The word occurs with revealing regularity throughout *Le Miroir des limbes* and would certainly figure at the head of any comprehensive analysis of the significant vocabulary of the book, together, not surprisingly, with others such as "transcender" and "métamorphose," similarly impregnated with *le sacré malrucien*.

So far this attempt to trace the outline of an expression of transcendence has been limited primarily to structural and lexical considerations. But much substance can be gleaned too from examination of the figurative level of the book. There, even more so than in the novels, one can point to a symbolic backdrop, both historical and geographical, which seeks by an intricate tissue of references to extend beyond any particularity the significance of both dialogue and circumstance. Having noted in passing a continuing predilection for certain adjectives like "mérovingien" and "moyenâgeux," we could select, as two examples among a multitude, first the passage where the women from Toulouse scream out the "Marseillaise": "ce n'était pas le chant solennel des prisonnières au moment du départ pour le camp d'extermination, c'était le hurlement que l'on entendit peut-être quand les femmes de Paris marchèrent sur Versailles,"[11] and second:

les bûches de Bénarès [qui] se reflétaient dans le fleuve comme se reflétaient dans l'Hudson glacé les lumières carrées de New York verticale sous les rafales de neige. Au dessus des forêts africaines, les arbres géants des Reines montaient vers les étoiles. Depuis cinquante siècles, le même silence où retombaient les bruits perdus recouvrait les hommes accordés par le sommeil à la terre nocturne – couchés, comme les morts.[12]

Against this symbolic background there move characters who are themselves beyond history, who are typified rather by "une certaine forme de grandeur irréelle."[13] Mao thus becomes an "empereur de bronze" whose ideas generate a veneration which resembles "plus à celle de la révélation du Prophète, qu'au sentiment que nous inspirent les grandes figures de notre histoire."[14] Nehru, we learn, perceives himself as "un maillon de cette chaîne ininterrompue qui prend ses racines, à l'aube de l'Histoire, dans notre passé immémorial"; and de Gaulle appears to his former comrade as "la dernière métamorphose du mythe de la France."[15] With all three, as with so many others, equally "transcendent" – such as Clappique, Madame Khodari Pacha, Senghor – the dialogue goes on.

And it is dialogue, throughout, that is the essential situation; a dialogue that is perhaps, in the final analysis, a dialogue between Malraux and himself. For we are confronted with a dialogue that is recognizable primarily for the uniformity of its tone, as a single consciousness tirelessly questions itself about destiny. Rather than discourse or exchange, we are dealing with a sort of dialogue between Siamese twins; indeed Malraux himself goes so far as to admit the univocal nature of his conversation with de Gaulle: "Il ne s'agit pas essentiellement d'un dialogue entre lui et moi, mais à travers moi, d'un dialogue en lui, l'histoire, les arbres, la nuit, la neige."

Still more remarkable are those occasions designated as "Oraisons funèbres" when Malraux communicates, or rather communes, in unforgettable fashion with an attendant collectivity. Who could have failed to be affected by the extraordinary magic of that day when Malraux spoke in order to commemorate the transfer of Jean Moulin's ashes to the Pantheon. Far more than any mere historical or geographical re-situating, we are faced on such an occasion with a qualitative shift from the circumstantial to the legendary. Paul-Henri Simon explains thus the necessary strategy and experience of a speaker in such a context: "s'en éloigner … prendre les événements et les hommes à un niveau symbolique où tout devient grandeur et signe, où la contingence et la médiocrité s'effacent devant une sublime intention qui donne un sens à la destinée."[17]

Although I am principally concerned here with Malraux's attempt in Le Miroir des limbes to fashion a mode of literary expression which was appropriate to a prevailing, if tentative, awareness of transcendence, it may be worth making passing reference to his parallel and contemporaneous effort to achieve similar effects through the medium of television. Already Malraux's abiding interest in the renewal of creative expression had allowed him to grasp far more quickly than most – as early as the 1920s – the importance of the new cinematographic art, and of the audiovisual onslaught in general. It is not surprising, therefore, that Malraux was extremely keen in 1971 to try to transpose to the screen the considerable harvest of his latest meditations.

Claude Santelli, the eventual producer of the series, confirms that the idea of *La Légende du siècle*, a delightfully Hugoesque title, was Malraux's own: "Et c'est André Malraux qui a exprimé le désir de faire quelque chose de plus vaste, de plus dense, quelque chose qui ait de plus grandes dimensions. Il souhaitait par la télévision créer des *Antimémoires* illustrées."[18] It would be clearly impractical and unfruitful to try to determine within the programs the respective contributions of Malraux and Santelli, and for this reason the nine episodes of *La Légende du siècle* only afford a footnote in any consideration of Malraux's narrative style. Nevertheless one can say with complete conviction that his commitment to the venture was enormous. Claude Santelli again offers his testimony: "Avec nos caméras, notre équipe, nous sommes allés pendant six mois, à partir d'avril 1971, dans sa propriété deux après-midis par semaine ... le dernier jour, il était si habitué à nous voir venir qu'il nous a dit, 'Vous partez? Déjà?'"[19]

Moreover, it was Malraux who personally chose the actors, Jean Vilar, Michel Bouquet, and Alain Cuny, who were to read the extracts from the novels. He also involved himself in all the creative selection and editing right up to the final montage, in which the "architecture" of *Le Miroir des limbes* must have been a decisive factor if one judges by evident similarities between the two works. For, according to Santelli, the television broadcasts were for Malraux "une forme de testament," in which the latter's principal preoccupation was "la quête de la religion," and for which there needed to be achieved an appropriate stylistic tone. This tone, just as in *Le Miroir des limbes*, was to be "lyrico-mythique."[20]

The links between the televisual creation and the literary one are frequently explicit – the same novelistic passages, the same speeches, the same subjects of conversation. We even discover that certain of the television episodes further expropriate titles that originally belonged to the novels before thereafter being borrowed for *Le Miroir des limbes*.

There is also an evident structural similarity. *La Légende du siècle* reveals the same sort of knowing collage effect, which fuses past and present, reality and fiction; a succession, contextualized but only in the loosest associative way, of newsreel or film clips, prints, readings, recordings, reminiscences, music, conversations, old photographs, and so on. Devices in a very different medium, but which produce an almost identical tone and confirm the aesthetic importance which Malraux attached to *Le Miroir des limbes*.

It is worth recalling that the point of convergence of all that is examined above is the author's wish to express that which transcends both the banality of the "état civil" and the fantasy of pure fiction. It is

Michel Droit's marvellously rich 1967 interview with Malraux which establishes beyond any doubt just such a primacy. To the question "Qu'est-ce qui compte, finalement?" Malraux replies: "La transcendance. La notion de transcender. Ce qui s'oppose à la servitude humaine"[21] – "servitude" signifying in Malraux's lexicon the human condition itself.

While recognizing Malraux's desire to inscribe the human adventure into a wider framework, but restricting themselves to domains such as revolution, art, and history, some critics have perhaps neglected the degree to which Malraux is instinctively religious, haunted above all by yearnings for some absolute. In a Godless world, deprived of any truly supreme values, divinity henceforth belongs to man. It would not be unreasonable to contend that Malraux from his earliest beginnings unflinchingly and unswervingly pursued an extended metaphysical reflection on the mortal destiny of the human species, and that it is this which finally determined his narrative evolution. Such a proposal would certainly go a long way towards explaining why anything remotely resembling imaginative writing was totally abandoned in the wake of *Les Noyers de l'Altenburg*.[22] This work, so long dismissed by the critics, should now perhaps be recognized, not as the second-rate offering of an out-of-breath novelist, but rather as prophetic – an attempt, at that point incomplete, to find a new form. Certainly, although a further twenty-five years of enrichment and maturation were required for fruition, already in the embryonic *Les Noyers de l'Altenburg* one can point to many of the devices which will eventually characterize the later *Miroir des limbes*: associationism, parallel structures, extensive dialogue, temporal interplay, stereoscopic juxtaposition. Thus Malraux's rejection of the novel after 1943, reconsidered in the illumination provided by *Le Miroir des limbes*, becomes merely a temporary hiatus in the face of the difficulty of forging a transcendental mode of expression, before the ultimate climactic accomplishment. It is the halting progress towards that accomplishment, over a period of some fifty years, which will be probed in the remaining chapters.

CHAPTER TWO

On the Present Tense

On peut analyser la mise en scène d'un
grand romancier. Que son objet soit le
récit de faits, la peinture ou l'analyse
de caractères, voire une interrogation
sur le sens de la vie; que son talent
tende à une prolifération, comme celui
de Hemingway, ou à une cristallisation
comme celui de Proust, il est amené ...
à rendre présent. (Malraux, "Esquisse d'une
psychologie du cinéma," 331)[1]

Although it is not particularly original to observe that the large majority of Malraux studies have concerned themselves primarily with his vision of the world – be it spiritual, social, or political – such an observation should perhaps disturb us more than it seems to. For Malraux, from his very first appearance on the literary and cultural scene, continuously demonstrated an intense preoccupation with art, with style, and with structure. More specifically, he chose from the outset to be novelist rather than philosopher. Rare indeed, however, are those as acutely perceptive as Julien Green, who noted laconically in the first volume of his *Journal* as long ago as the early thirties: "27 mars – Déjeuner avec Malraux, à la Pergola, avenue du Maine. Il croit que je fais mes romans d'après des plans et suivant une technique bien raisonnée. Inutile d'expliquer."[2]

What Green apparently is suggesting is that, for Malraux, any other approach to writing a novel than a reasoned and concerted one is unimaginable. Certainly Malraux's scattered comments on the art of writing narrative, particularly in the still fascinating *Esquisse d'une psychologie du cinéma*, from which the exergual quotation was taken, confirm Green's impression of the personal tendencies of his erstwhile lunch companion.

Perhaps the principal early result of such attention to form within his novelistic expression is the evocation of immediacy, the convincing illusion of "being present." A Malraux novel, as distinct from those of many who had preceded him, is less a reading than an act; the recipient is no longer spectator but participant, for the author allows little or no distance – spatial or temporal – between the events of the narrative and the reading experience. We are not permitted that comfortable withdrawal which once enabled us to discover and contemplate in relative safety an author's world and preoccupations; we are confronted by circumstances in which we are virtual protagonists. This, for Malraux, is what has long determined the evolutionary process of the novel, and remains the goal – even more pointedly perhaps – today: "L'histoire de la technique du récit suit essentiellement la recherche d'une troisième dimension, de ce qui dans le roman échappe au récit, de ce qui permet, non de raconter, mais de représenter, de rendre présent."[3]

What is required is the presentation of an action that is almost palpable, that tears the recalcitrant reader from his old-fashioned armchair and thrusts him into the plot. Indeed, one can go still further: for Malraux *presence* seems to be quite essential to any work of art. It is by presence that a work of art is defined; that is the mysterious quality by which creative genius may be recognized. Symptomatically, on the very first page of *La Métamorphose des dieux*, Malraux elected to affirm:

Les hommes pour qui l'art existe ne s'unissent point par leur raffinement ou leur éclectisme, mais par leur reconnaissance du mystérieux pouvoir qui rend *présentes* à leurs yeux telles peintures préhistoriques dont le mot magie n'explique nullement les formes, les statues sumériennes dont ils ne connaissent guère les noms, et LA DAME D'ELCHE dont ils ignorent tout.[4]

It is this extensive and vigorous insistence on the primacy of presence in effective artistic expression that invites us to examine in Malraux's writings the most fundamental means of achieving immediacy in narrative – the present tense.

It should be asserted from the outset that there is no naïve suggestion here that, in itself, the use of the present tense by Malraux was particularly innovative; on the contrary, the practice may well be considered banal. Several are the writers prior to Malraux who have profited from such an expedient in order to render capital events more dramatically. There is no doubt that a glance through any small library would turn up many examples like that of a famous nineteenth-century historian who required recourse to that very device in his description of the siege of the Bastille:

Le sang coule, nouvel aliment à la fureur. Les blessés sont portés dans les maisons de la rue de la Cerisaie; les mourants laissent comme dernière recommandation de ne pas céder, de combattre jusqu'à la chute du fort maudit. Mais comment hélas! le faire? Les murs sont si épais! Des députations, jusqu'à trois, arrivent de l'hôtel de ville.[5]

This partial use of the present tense, inserted for effect into a narrative that is for the most part in the past, becomes even more prevalent at about the time Malraux was beginning to write. There is, for instance, *Le Diable au corps* by Radiguet in which the story becomes "present" at the moment when the couple make love for the first time:

J'en voulais à Marthe, parce que je comprenais, à son visage reconnaissant, tout ce que valent les liens de la chair. Je maudissais l'homme qui avait avant moi éveillé son corps...

Maintenant nous pleurons ensemble; c'est la faute du bonheur. Marthe me reproche de n'avoir pas empêché son mariage.[6]

But, despite the fact that such examples do abound, the appearance of the present tense as the narrative tense for the entire duration of Malraux's first novel, *Les Conquérants*, remains important. It serves both as an early signpost to what may possibly be the principal aesthetic preoccupation of the author, and also to mark the initial point in an itinerary which, through its tense modifications, will gradually reveal the growing refinement of the author's vehicle.

It is probably unnecessary to recall that the specific intent of the present tense is the suppression of the temporal distance which traditionally separates the imaginary action from its recounting: that is, the events, the images, the dialogue, spring up before us as if we were there. Thus, in *Les Conquérants*, the reader is propelled into the crucial battle between the cadets and the anti-insurgency troops of General Tang; he is "technically" in the streets where the events are occurring. Indeed, as I noted earlier, the present tense is utilized from the first page of the novel as the reader is plunged into the midst of the shipboard passengers studying the latest news bulletin to be posted:

La grève générale est décrétée à Canton. Depuis hier, ce radio est affiché, souligné en rouge. Jusqu'à l'horizon, l'océan indien immobile, glacé, laqué – sans sillages. Le ciel plein de nuages fait peser sur nous une atmosphère de cabines de bain, nous entoure d'air saturé. Et les passagers marchent, à pas comptés, sur le pont, se gardant bien de s'éloigner du cadre blanc dans lequel vont être fixés les radios reçus cette nuit.[7]

Immediacy? Yes, but the question that needs, of course, to be asked is whether the effect would not have been greater had Malraux restricted his use of the device solely to the really significant and dramatic moments of the novel. The quality of immediacy that theoretically characterizes this tense may well be diminished because at no point is it contrasted with a narrative in the past. The reader becomes accustomed, and may well cease to register – at least in any vivid way – the immediacy, the unrelenting tension, that is being sought.

That Malraux was not unaware of these limitations is clearly suggested by the almost total disappearance of the present tense from the two novels which followed, *La Voie royale* and *La Condition humaine*. There does occur, admittedly, an isolated instance of free direct style, an infinitive, within the more general predilection for free indirect style which, at least provisionally, seems to be preferred in the quest for immediacy. Tchen, the protagonist, is about to strike the form sleeping beneath the mosquito netting, but is delayed by a moment of compulsive reflection:

Quatre ou cinq klaxons grincèrent à la fois. *Découvert? Combattre, combattre, des ennemis éveillés!*

La vague de vacarme retomba: quelque embarras de voitures (il y avait encore des embarras de voitures, là-bas, dans le monde des hommes...).[8]

But such an example is almost unique, and it is only in 1935 with the publication of *Le Temps du mépris* that Malraux returns to any extensive use of the present tense.

It is in the third chapter that we discover to what a considerable degree the somewhat crude ubiquity of this tense in *Les Conquérants* has now been substantially modified. The present tense is now re-situated within an interlaced network of tenses, which seeks to represent stylistically Kassner's vacillations between insanity and reality. The reader has learned at the end of the preceding chapter that Kassner is concerned about his wavering mental stability, and is determined to make a supreme effort of will to control this incipient madness: "Une chasse vertigineuse lançait son esprit vers les images qui maintenaient sa vie. Il fallait organiser cette chasse, la transformer en volonté."[9]

The deliberateness and importance of Kassner's reaction is restated at the start of the third chapter: "L'esprit de Kassner tournait dans l'évasion comme son corps dans la cellule. Il fallait se souvenir minutieusement, reconstituer avec application. Non pas être emporté: recréer."[10] Because of such reiteration it would seem reasonable to contend that Malraux is here seeking to establish the intricate enormity of the contest that is about to take place between a rational mind and an irrational situation. It is significant for the present study that the movements and stages of the struggle that does indeed ensue are conveyed by a complex series of tense changes, in which the present tense plays its considerable part. In fact, of the twelve changes of narrative tense that take place within the third chapter, six involve the present tense – a present tense used, at different points in Kassner's descent into his own cerebral vortex, to translate actual memories, the reality of the cell, and even, towards the end, the vivid fantasies of a mind provisionally out of control.[11]

The virtuosity of this extraordinary manipulation of tenses is striking, but it is difficult to imagine a circumstance other than this borderline of reality and unreality that could take advantage of such interweaving. It is not surprising, therefore, that Malraux demonstrates in *L'Espoir* a somewhat more discreet use of the potentiality of the present tense than either that of *Les Conquérants* or *Le Temps du mépris*. In fact, so discreet are its appearances[12] that, although it does manifest itself on ten occasions to communicate with greater emphasis and force the truly decisive moments of the action, these occurrences have gone largely unnoticed, and certainly unremarked upon, by commentators. For this reason it may be useful to chronicle the episodes that are singled out in this way and to indicate their particular content:

1   *L'illusion lyrique II* – chap. 5 (pp. 88–91)
    The organization of the Republican army.
2   *L'exercice de l'apocalypse II* – chap. 7 (pp. 228–35)
    The dynamiters against the Fascist tanks.
3   *L'exercice de l'apocalypse II* – chap. 10 (pp. 252–7)
    The death of Hernandez.
4   *Le manzanarès (être et faire) I* – chap. 2 (pp. 271–3)
    Magnin's airplane caught in the searchlight.
5   *Le manzanarès (être et faire) I* – chap. 8 (pp. 322–5)
    Preparations for the defence of Madrid.
6   *Le manzanarès (être et faire) I* – chap. 9 (pp. 326–32)
    The first combat of the International brigade.
7   *Le manzanarès (sang de gauche)* – chap. 3 (pp. 342–3)
    The three Germans and their wounded comrade.
8   *Le manzanarès (sang de gauche)* – chap. 14 (pp. 396–8)
    The arrival of the Russian planes.
9   *Le manzanarès (sang de gauche)* – chap. 17 (pp. 406–13)
    The success of the Republican counter-offensive.
10 *L'espoir I* – chap. 3 (pp. 474–5)
    The descent of the wounded aviators.

The importance that Malraux continues, at this relatively late point in his novelistic career, to attach to the present tense would seem to be evident from the subject-matter which it is chosen to express. For the passages listed above are without doubt among the most significant of the novel. Moreover, it is not solely to convey the immediacy of a climactic moment of the action that this tense is employed, although this certainly remains valid on such occasions as the arrival of the Russian planes:

Les obus éclatent, dans l'indifférence générale. A chaque obus proche, dans la boîte, un ou deux papillons tombent.

Manuel écrit une phrase dans la marge d'une carte d'état-major, déployée sur la table devant lui.

Gartner le regarde, regarde chacun de ses camarades; sa bouche petite dans son visage plat avale tout à coup sa salive et dit enfin, du ton dont on annonce la victoire, la défaite ou la paix:

"Camarades, les avions russes sont arrivés."[13]

Elsewhere, however, it may rather be a predominant theme that is placed in relief by such tense utilization. This is the case with regard to the *fraternité virile* which characterizes the relationship between Siry and Kogan as, during the first combat experience of the International brigade, they manage to communicate, but only through whistles:

Un chant de merle s'élève, reste suspendu comme une question, – un autre lui répond. Le premier reprend, pose une question plus inquiète; le second proteste furieusement, et des éclats de rire passent à travers la brume. "T'as raison, dit une voix: passeront pas. Des clous!" Les merles sont Siry et Kogan, de la première brigade internationale. Kogan est bulgare, et ne sait pas le français: ils sifflent.[14]

A very different usage is to be found in the description of Hernandez's execution. There we are confronted less by a conventional dramatization – thematic or circumstantial – although clearly this is in no way excluded, than by the total identification of readers and prisoners. So much so in fact that the prisoners' error of perception becomes transferred to the readers who, given no distance, have no possibility of recognizing or correcting an imperfect vision:

Trois fascistes viennent prendre trois prisonniers. Ils les mènent devant la fosse, reculent. – En joue! ...

Ils font un saut périlleux en arrière. Le peloton tire, mais ils sont déjà dans la fosse. Comment peuvent-ils espérer s'en échapper? Les prisonniers rient nerveusement.

Ils n'auront pas à s'en échapper. Les prisonniers ont vu le saut d'abord, mais le peloton a tiré avant. Les nerfs.[15]

This deliberate fusion of the characters' perceptions with the readers', regardless of any objective validity, in the unremitting actuality of the present, is perhaps the most striking use of the present tense to be found in Malraux's writings. Certainly the discretion and range of its utilization throughout *L'Espoir* point to a far more refined awareness of its varying value than that revealed previously.

In his final novel, *Les Noyers de l'Altenburg*, Malraux retains the present tense for both the first and third parts of the work. There, at a superficial level, it communicates the relative closeness of the events being described, as distinct from the historical distance that marks the central section of the text. Moreover, since we are dealing with a kind of diary, in those parts the chosen tense also brings out the vividness of personal recollection. But perhaps the most interesting possibility is that this tense is endowed here with a gnomic quality that adds yet another facet to Malraux's exploitation of the technique. In this way it would inform the fundamental historico-cultural conviction that underpins the work – namely the continuity and universality of mankind. Present in the mystical and figurative certainty that Vincent Berger's walnut trees oppose to Möllberg's theoretical arguments, present too in the connective tissue of historical and geographical allusion ("massive babylonienne," "visages gothiques," "momies," "voix préhistoriques," "Arabes," "Sénégalais," "Loire," "Allemands," "Bretagne," "Pérou"), this conviction acquires still further substance by the most eternal of tenses. Reiterated sentences such as "c'est le moyen âge" become therefore the very crystallization of an overall tendency through their amalgamation of past reference and present tense.[16] Once again Malraux contrives to reinforce his subject-matter by an apparently simple device that can now be seen to be remarkably multifaceted.

Of course, in the final analysis, what is important in the above is not so much any new discovery with regard to the values of the present tense, but the fact that Malraux does explore assiduously the entire range. For that fact has not, it would seem, been sufficiently emphasized to date. And yet it affords one more confirmation, among a growing number, of the degree to which Malraux the novelist must be re-situated among those whose works are significant, not only for what they seek to say, but also – and perhaps above all – for the manner in which they elect to say it. It is this concern for expression which we shall continue to investigate in the subsequent chapters.

CHAPTER THREE

On Eroticism

il s'agit ... de faire de notre
conscience érotique, dans ce qu'elle
a de plus viril, le système de références
de notre vie. (Malraux, "Préface" to
D.H. Lawrence, *L'Amant de Lady
Chatterley*, ii)

In 1933 André Malraux was awarded the Prix Goncourt for a novel, *La
Condition humaine*, in which a major theme – possibly *the* theme which
reverberates most widely throughout the novel, essentially in Ferral,
Valérie, and Clappique, but also metaphorically in Tchen and
reflectively in Gisors – is that of eroticism. In fact, so powerful was the
compulsion to communicate the *meaningful* nature of the erotic act that
Malraux was at pains to eliminate one chapter concerning Clappique,
subsequently published separately in the periodical *Marianne*,[1]
probably in part because its voyeuristic overtones were too facile and
callow for his purpose. And yet prior to 1933, in a literary career
already spanning some thirteen years, this same theme, although
present, was never more than, at most, allusive or embryonic.

Indeed, in the *écrits farfelus* which occupied his early years there is
very little evidence of any real value attached to eroticism. Only in
Lunes en papier does one discover a certain literary titillation as,
infrequently, *ludique* gently nudges *lubrique*:

La Luxure s'était enfuie avec le musicien, et le profil de leurs jambes
obscènement enlacées séparait en deux croissants inégaux le morceau de ciel
contenu dans l'une des lucarnes, "Elle est bien dépourvue de sainteté, en
vérité, poursuivit l'Orgueil. Qu'il lui est utile d'être un péché pour être si peu
blasée! Et puis voyons, voyons, son sexe actuel, qui est le masculin, doit être
gênant; il n'est peut-être pas pédéraste, ce jeune confrère. Il est vrai qu'il est
devenu l'Envie. Cela est sujet à de nombreuses réflexions, que je ne
manquerai pas de faire plus tard.[2]

But such playfulness is of no more genuine substance than the curious "erotica" that Malraux was helping to publish at this same period "under the counter" for Kra.[3]

By 1926, however, in *La Tentation de l'Occident*, the confrontation of Eastern and Western values that determines the epistolary structure of this book allowed Malraux to make early, but telling, statements concerning the role of the imagination in the elevation of the purely sexual to the erotic. But the as-yet-inconclusive nature of these observations at this time is attested by their lack of development in the novel which followed in 1928, *Les Conquérants*. There we encounter only Rebecci's mildly perverted fantasies and Garine's occasional therapeutic exor- (or, if you prefer, exer-) -cising:

Il [Rebecci] vivait entouré de petites filles qu'il avait recueillies, servantes dont le principal travail était d'écouter des histoires, et que surveillait avec soin son épouse chinoise qui n'ignorait pas qu'il eût été curieux de tenter avec elles quelques expériences. Hanté par un érotisme de colonial, il ne quittait *Les clavicules de Salomon* que pour lire ou relire *Le règne du fouet, Esclave* ou quelque autre livre français du même genre.[4]

And Garine, discovered in the act, so to speak, explains thus to the narrator: "Lorsqu'on est ici depuis un certain temps, me dit-il dans l'escalier, les Chinoises énervent beaucoup, tu verras. Alors pour s'occuper en paix de choses sérieuses, le mieux est de coucher avec elles et de n'y plus penser."[5]

Certainly, there is nothing here either to announce the depth and proliferation that will characterize the erotic theme in *La Condition humaine*. Not even *La Voie royale* in 1930 allows us to anticipate the extent of the role to be attributed to eroticism some three years later. None the less, in that volume certain contours are beginning to emerge. The erotic *is* serious, as suggested during Claude's account of a recent visit to a Somali brothel: "La patronne avait poussé vers Perken une fille toute jeune, qui souriait. Non, dit-il; l'autre là-bas. Au moins ça n'a pas l'air de l'amuser."[6]

The erotic is also depersonalized in its nature, self-fulfilling in its intent: "L'essentiel est de *ne pas connaître* la partenaire. Qu'elle soit: l'autre sexe."[7] In addition, it would seem doomed to failure: "Jamais il ne trouverait dans cette frénésie qui le secouait autre chose que la pire des séparations."[8] But these and other fragments, although prophetic, remain subordinate in a novel dominated by the broader theme of Perken's mythomanic desire to realize all the fabrications of his imagination. It is *only* in *La Condition humaine* that the erotic is finally fleshed out, established as fundamental to any understanding of Malraux's vision of the world. Indeed, it is not unreasonable to contend that a remarkable growth, both qualitative and quantitative, has occurred between 1930 and 1933, which has invested the theme we are considering with a new and dramatic potential for illumination.

What can explain this development? What event or events have taken place in this intervening period which might have had a profound effect on Malraux?

I should like to postulate that the only plausible explanation may well be Malraux's reading in 1931–2 of D.H. Lawrence, especially of *Lady Chatterley's Lover*. Although this work had appeared in English in Paris in 1928, Malraux discovered it in 1931 while working for Gallimard, which was preparing the first French translation. In fact he was sufficiently taken with the work to write the "Préface" for that edition, which finally appeared early in 1932. It is examination of this preface, for the most part, which suggests the degree to which reflection on Lawrence's novel allowed Malraux to focus and explore his notion of the erotic, and to attain the perspective which will be his own in *La Condition humaine*.

In particular, in this preface of some four and a half pages, Malraux discusses two aspects he feels are emphatically key aspects in Lawrence's work: first, eroticism as the ultimately meaningful human experience and, second, eroticism as just as much a female experience as male, with woman no longer cast as mere container. At the beginning of the preface, having cursorily traced the evolution of attitudes towards eroticism through the centuries, Malraux stresses the expansion that Lawrence's writings demonstrate: "Il [l'érotisme] était le diable, il devient l'homme; nous allons le voir dépasser l'homme, devenir sa raison d'être,"[9] even to the point that we should "en faire le moyen de notre propre révélation... il s'agit d'être homme – le plus possible. C'est-à-dire de faire de notre conscience érotique, dans ce qu'elle a de plus viril, le système de références de notre vie."[10]

In this guise, then, eroticism becomes the supreme act in a world now dominated by a very mortal, and therefore, physical man – *or* woman – for Malraux is struck too by the resoluteness with which Lawrence rejects the conventional, impoverishing, stylization of woman. Even the Christian, suggests Malraux, should feel chastised by Lawrence for an adherence to a certain "éternel féminin": "Jamais le chrétien n'a vu dans la femme un être tout à fait humain."[11]

Certainly, it cannot be denied that Lawrence, already ravaged by disease to the point of imminent death, did choose to devote his last major work primarily to a woman's sensuality: "Il l'interroge par la voix de tous ses personnages et lui consacre le livre qu'il écrit lorsqu'il est déjà fasciné par la mort,"[12] writes Malraux, for whom it is undoubtedly Constance who subsumes even Mellors in her erotic itinerary:

il fallait que les rapports entre elle et son nouvel amant fussent impersonnels, il fallait qu'elle devînt sa maîtresse avant de savoir qui il est, avant de lui avoir parlé. De quoi a-t-elle besoin? De se révéler à elle-même à l'aide de sa propre sexualité. Peu importe le moyen de cet éveil. Que Mellors se réduise d'abord à un sexe adroit et anonyme: qu'il ne soit, à aucun titre, le séducteur, le vrai dialogue est entre Lady Chatterley et elle-même.[13]

These then are the principal elements Malraux points to in his preface to Lawrence's work; these are also the pivotal elements in the new value which will be invested in the erotic in *La Condition humaine*.

It would, of course, be naïve to suggest that Malraux takes from Lawrence any more than a new, and largely interrogative, awareness of how *fundamental* the erotic experience may be for *all* human beings. Lawrence is primarily a stimulus, not a source. The differences between the two should not be glossed over, for they are considerable. Indeed, Elizabeth Tenenbaum in her book *The Problematic Self: Approaches to Identity in Stendhal, D.H. Lawrence and Malraux* goes so far as to affirm that in fact Lawrence and Malraux each espouse one of two diametrically opposed Romantic perspectives: Lawrence projecting "a Romantic celebration of a natural impulsive self" and Malraux proposing a "Romantic commitment to the volitional creation of a freely-chosen identity."[14] I would prefer not to draw the lines quite so boldly. In both, for example, there are sequences which seem at least to investigate the possibility that human fulfilment requires a sense of organic (sic) connection to a world *beyond* the self.

Be that as it may, there remain far-reaching differences. For Lawrence, in *Lady Chatterley's Lover*, the exaltation of one's sensuality, the restoration of the "natural flow," does seem to be *successful* revitalization in the face of unnaturalness and human solitude; whereas for Malraux, in part, such an exercise may be an act of aggression – akin even to murder and terrorism – an attempt to demonstrate one's power to dominate the world around and, thereby, affirm one's own uniqueness, but an attempt that is inevitably, despite fleeting gratification, doomed to failure.

Moreover, a further general qualitative distinction imposes itself. There is in Malraux a desensitization of the erotic, be it translated by the unwavering lucidity of Ferral or by the unrestrained rutting of Clappique (three times in half an hour in the original manuscript, computes Frohock),[15] a desensitization that invokes an *affective* barren-ness far removed from the sensual and vital awareness of Lawrence. It is in part this devaluation of the affective which elevates (or relegates, if one prefers) the erotic in Malraux to the level of the cerebral, as he is the first to recognize: "C'est une idée de toute évidence."[16]

One discovers precisely the reverse in *Lady Chatterley's Lover*, where Clifford, who insistently conceptualizes all experience, "turn-ing everything into words,"[17] is presented as ineffectual and devoid of real life. It is Lady Chatterley, of course, who enunciates the fundamental credo:

I believe the life of the body is a greater reality than the life of the mind: when the body is really wakened to life ... The human body is only just coming to real life. With the Greeks it gave a lovely flicker, then Plato and Aristotle killed it, and Jesus finished it off. But now the body is coming really to life, it is really rising from the tomb. And it will be a lovely, lovely life in the lovely universe, the life of the human body.[18]

It has been suggested too, by Anaïs Nin in her so-called "Unprofes-sional Study" of D.H. Lawrence, that the much-publicized crudeness in the book serves deliberately to dethrone mentally directed love, to facilitate a return to the basic and instinctive: "A language to renew contact with the reality of sexual passion, distorted by the cult of idealism."[19]

Having broached parenthetically such general differences, let me now return to my thesis that, *nevertheless*, Malraux's reading of Lawrence in 1931–2 was crucial to the importance and meaning he was to attach to the erotic in *La Condition humaine*. For, differences and reservations notwithstanding, and as I have already indicated, Malraux is very definite in his preface both about the enormous significance of the erotic as an avenue which merits full exploration, and about the validity of such exploration for man *and* woman.

Undoubtedly, the key sequence in this respect in *La Condition humaine* is the one which brings together Ferral and Valérie. There, the working out in novelistic form of what Malraux seems to have distilled from his meditation on Lawrence culminates in what may well be the most succinct and exemplary formulation of Malraux's tragic vision – I refer to the little discussed Tibetan banner which, towards the end of the novel, serves as a backcloth to the human coupling on the bed below: "Il [Ferral] regarda la peinture thibétaine: sur un monde décoloré où erraient des voyageurs, deux squelettes exactement semblables s'étreignaient en transe. Il s'approcha de la femme."[20] Quantitatively remarkable relative to any previous descriptions, the Ferral-Valérie sequence occupies some thirty pages of the Folio edition as it proceeds from the first sexual encounter, to the caricatural sequel of the birds in Valérie's hotel room, through its explication and generalization by Gisors, to the symbolic climax in the artistic image of that Tibetan painting, as Ferral seeks provisional relief in yet another body.

The special quality of this particular relationship seems to derive from the impressive presence of Valérie. Far more than the mere recipient or faceless prostitute who had previously appeared in Malraux's novels, from her first appearance in the text she is presented as Ferral's equal. She is proud, rich, independent, and intelligent, with a rare gift for aphorism; she is in no way daunted by her male partner: "Croyez-vous que ce n'est pas l'histoire du bouchon qui se croyait tellement plus important que la bouteille?"[21] she asks. Ferral himself admits that in some ways Valérie's nature is very comparable to his own: "Elle se sent en fonction de son sexe comme moi en fonction du mien, ni plus ni moins."[22] Indeed, Ferral goes on to affirm specifically *her* independence, identical to his own: "Un être humain, pensa Ferral, une vie individuelle, isolée, unique comme la mienne."[23]

It is, then, between these two characters, whose similarity is clear and explicit, that there exists the most developed erotic relationship to be found in Malraux's writings. And yet for both the experience is frustrating. Neither finds any real satisfaction in the other, neither makes any new discovery in the self. The final rejection is both lucid and mutual.

It is this erotic encounter which is contextualized by the potentiality of the two identical skeletons intertwined on the Tibetan wall-hanging over Ferral's bed. Devoid of detail and devoid of flesh, they serve to bestow on the carnal coupling about to take place below a symbolic quality that is both impersonal and de-sexualized. Eroticism, for Malraux, is in all ways, and always, an ultimately negative and unfulfilling experience.

But should we go further in our conclusions? Certainly, Malraux's preface to *Lady Chatterley's Lover*, as we have already observed, invites us to attempt to discover in the erotic "le moyen de notre propre révélation," "le système de références de notre vie," and certainly the plastic and iconographic resonance of the Tibetan banner is extremely provocative.

Moreover, the link between Eros and Thanatos has long been characteristic of many cultures, and has been expressed in many art forms. More precisely, and more appositely for our present pre-occupations, it is a link which Tchen recalls explicitly in the dialogue of *La Condition humaine*. For him someone who has never killed is to be identified with a virgin. "Ceux qui ne tuent pas: les puceaux," he replies to one of Gisors' questions.[24] It may well be that for Malraux, in 1933, the erotic act, *la petite mort*, is regarded as the most fundamental and exemplary of mortal experiences; the one which more than any other epitomizes man's desperate quest in a now Godless world where Death is terribly final. Thus, if Ferral's imminent embracing of yet another courtesan may be taken to denote his continuing desire for some form of human transcendence, then his brief glimpse of the Tibetan painting evokes the inevitability of his failure to attain.

In the wake of a secular Armageddon, in a world of deflated myths and shattered traditions, there were many attempts to express in literature some new and positive value in a now very physical man. It is my contention that Malraux's reading of Lawrence, as evinced in his 1932 preface to the first French translation of *Lady Chatterley's Lover*, encouraged him to explore, along specific lines and more substantially than might otherwise have been the case, one particular avenue. His exploration is both exhaustive and exhausting. There is *no* solace in that direction, and eroticism will not reappear in *any* form in *any* of his subsequent writings. In this sense Malraux's reflective mating with Lawrence in 1932 is a perfect image of the erotic act itself, at least for Malraux. Orgasmic at the time, but very soon over.

CHAPTER FOUR

On Free Indirect Style

la voie royale est manifestement
de pousser le lecteur à la complicité.
(Malraux, *L'Homme précaire et la littérature*, 196)[1]

Malraux's commitment to the realization of the illusion of immediacy in his novels has already been investigated in an earlier chapter with regard to the present tense. Although, as we have seen, that particular device, utilized throughout *Les Conquérants*, is continued in intermittent form thereafter, Malraux also exploits to the same end, and with considerable effect, a further device, that of free indirect style.

Free indirect style avoids many of the restrictions and pitfalls of the somewhat cruder devices of present tense and first person narratives, but retains for the reader the advantages of virtually direct access to a character's thoughts, thereby compelling a greater involvement in the plot. It is perhaps worth underlining in passing that the presence of such a level of discourse in literature was only recognized formally by the linguists a few years prior to Malraux's first ventures into the arena of writing. It was the Swiss scholar, Bally, in 1909, who initially postulated the existence of a style beyond the consecrated levels of direct and indirect speech. Citing Flaubert as the great innovator in this regard, with La Fontaine as a noteworthy precursor, Bally explains[2] that free indirect style possesses aspects from each of the more traditional forms: from indirect or reported speech it retains the delicate system of transposition of verbs and pronouns, and from direct speech it retains the absence of explicit subordination ("Il dit que..." etc.). Moreover, free indirect style preserves those affective elements which are sacrificed in normal reported speech, as well as the questions and exclamations which are also part of the essential subjective texture of any utterance or thought.

Of course the attraction of such a technique for an author whose avowed aesthetic goals privilege the presence and participation of the reader is evident. Nor is there any doubt that free indirect style and its more blatant companion, *monologue intérieur*, were part of the literary climate which prevailed during Malraux's formative years in Paris; Joyce, Valéry Larbaud, Gide, and a host of others bear unequivocal witness to this.

It is in Malraux's second novel, *La Voie royale*, that free indirect style occurs for the first time in that writer's work. There, for the most part, it is to Claude's thoughts that the reader is given in this way almost unfiltered access:

Il se retourna vers Perken, interrogatif. – Ils plantent des lancettes de guerre.

Donc ils attendaient bien la nuit, et prenaient leurs précautions. Et combien de travaux semblables se préparaient ou se poursuivaient, derrière la case, derrière la ligne fourmillante de ces corps penchés?

Empêcher les Moïs d'incendier leur case, il n'y fallait pas songer: le feu allumé, ils ne pourraient que se lancer en avant – contre les arbalètes – ou à droite, vers les lancettes de guerre.[3]

In this passage, taken from the episode with the Moïs, the second and third paragraphs make use of the device we are examining in order to avoid the greater distancing that would have been occasioned by the repetition of expressions such as "Claude se disait que…" or "Claude se demandait si…" But, in *La Voie royale*, although extensively used, free indirect style offers little more than this ready confirmation of the author's general narrative preoccupations.

However, in the following novel, *La Condition humaine*, what was largely indicative becomes almost the keystone for the entire structure of the book. The reader enters directly and repeatedly into the mental continuum of each protagonist – Gisors, Kyo, Katow, Ferral, Clappique, Hemmelrich. Thus, in the early pages, it is Tchen's consciousness, as he stands hesitantly over his prospective victim, which provides the narrative – without the least commentary or observation by any external agent:

Un seul geste, et l'homme serait mort. Le tuer n'était rien: c'était le toucher qui était impossible. Et il fallait frapper avec précision. Le dormeur couché sur le dos, au milieu du lit à l'européenne, n'était habillé que d'un caleçon court, mais sous la peau grasse, les côtes n'étaient pas visibles.[4]

Although clearly we are not dealing here with the raw matter of the mental process – free indirect style gives only relative complicity through the imperfect or conditional tenses – there is, as we have already observed, a very marked reduction in the traditional distance between reader and fictional event.

Elsewhere, it is frequently Gisors, the intellectual centre of the work, who explains to himself, and to us, the psychology of those who gravitate around him. On this occasion it is Tchen who is evoked:

Gisors ... s'efforçait de se souvenir de l'adolescent d'alors ...

Dès qu'il avait observé Tchen, il avait compris que cet adolescent ne pouvait vivre d'une idéologie qui ne se transformât pas immédiatement en actes. Privé de charité, il ne pouvait être amené par la vie religieuse qu'à la contemplation ou à la vie intérieure; mais il haïssait la contemplation, et n'eût rêvé que d'un apostolat dont le rejetait précisément son absence de charité. Pour vivre il fallait donc d'abord qu'il échappât à son christianisme.[5]

The fragmentation or multiplicity of point of view that is achieved by such a device allows the reader to explore, more directly than would otherwise have been the case, the various human attitudes that are being projected and made explicit by the author. In fact it would not be too reckless a simplification to suggest that, in this novel, free indirect style is the most significant single technique on which Malraux relies to communicate the distinctness of the various elements in his tentative vision of mankind, those several psychologies which collectively justify the scope of the title itself.

Malraux's endorsement of free indirect style as a means by which to associate more closely reader and character continues in *Le Temps du mépris*. There, far from any fragmentation, however, for large parts of the narrative we are enclosed solely within the cranial cavity of the hero Kassner. From the very first moments of his interrogation, with which the book commences, our view is repeatedly limited to the character's:

Comme tous ceux qui ont parfois lieu de cacher leur identité, Kassner connaissait bien son long visage de cheval aux mâchoires serrées. Quelle photo l'hitlérien examinait-il? Kassner la voyait à l'envers. Pas très dangereuse: il était alors tondu, et l'impression de cet étroit masque tout en os, aux oreilles pointues, était passablement différente...[6]

On occasion in this novel free indirect style is modified and becomes, in the present tense, more akin to free *direct* style[7] as Kassner's imagination, increasingly vivid under the strain of incarceration and torture, is so presented to the reader:

Les popes sortis du tertre commencent à avancer, dalmatiques et tiares, sous les croix et les bannières, et une irréalité sans limites anime ce trésor en marche, cette folie d'orfèvre lachée dans les champs boueux, avec toutes les barbes blanches et ces tremblotants reflets de perles et d'argent sous la lune.

Ils approchent, en chantant avec une haine indignée la psalmodie qui depuis des heures rôde dans le cachot...[8]

These striking visions which animate Kassner's troubled mind are presented without any subordination, without any spatio-temporal distancing, in a form which is astride free indirect style and stream of consciousness. The result, in the first instance, would seem to be the happy realization of a still greater proximity between reader and story. But, in the final analysis, we are faced throughout the book with heavy doses of total interiorization within a single character which run counter to the universality of Malraux's announced theme: "tenter de donner conscience à des hommes de la grandeur qu'ils ignorent en eux."[9] It may be true, therefore, that Malraux, by simplifying and singularizing his focus and with it his use of free indirect style, so simplifies the structure that it becomes patently harmful and inadequate to carry the intended breadth of his vision. In this regard a letter from Malraux to his great friend Eddy du Perron is, I believe, apposite:

Plus ça va, plus je me rends compte de notre indifférence foncière à l'égard de ce que ces bonnes gens [les critiques] appellent "l'art du roman." *Adrienne Mesurat* est un chef d'œuvre, vous dit-on. C'est peu probable – mais si c'était vrai ça me ferait le même effet. Il y a des gens qui ont quelque chose à exprimer et qui ne font jamais des chefs d'œuvre – Montaigne, Pascal, Goya – parce qu'on ne domine pas une passion qui attaque le monde: et il y a ceux qui font des objets.[10]

In *Le Temps du mépris* Malraux seems to have fallen prey to the trap evoked in this letter and, by seeking too conscientiously to harness his subject to an "art de roman," to that distilled classical purity revered in his preface,[11] he merely fabricates an object. Certainly, free indirect style will appear much more sparingly in the works which follow.

In *L'Espoir*, in addition to the utilization I have already recorded as most generalized, we also discover that variant in the present tense which was noted with regard to *Le Temps du mépris*. Indeed, Malraux uses this latter version so forcefully on occasion that the reader's perspective is unremittingly riveted to that of a character recalling thereby, more dramatically than hitherto, Pouillon's elaboration of "la vision avec."[12] Not only does the reader then *perceive* events with the character in question, the reader may also be *deceived* with that character. In a kind of cinematographic *trompe l'oeil*, an optical illusion may thus masquerade as objective narrative. For example, in that poignant scene which I have already cited extensively in another context,[13] the extreme tension of the moment preceding the execution of Hernandez and his companions causes them – and us – to see that which is in fact not true. The degree of immediacy is remarkable, since the reader has to embrace not only the actual vision of the characters but also the hallucinatory creations of their imaginations.

Precisely the same device recurs in the last novel, *Les Noyers de l'Altenburg*, during the account of the Vistula gas attack. Vincent Berger, waiting anxiously for the return of his soldiers, is studying the Russian trenches:

Un homme en manches de chemises venait de sortir de la tranchée.

La forme blanche avança un peu. Quelle inexplicable marche: un homme de deux mètres, au tout petit buste presque horizontal. Il s'arrêta, tomba. Il y en avait un autre avec lui. Tout le long de la tranchée, des hommes en manches de chemise, taches blanches nettes malgré la distance, sortirent. Tous trop hauts, cahotants comme des géants de foire, se rompirent. La partie du corps en manches de chemise tomba; l'autre, le bas du corps, continua d'avancer. Ils étaient faits de deux hommes, l'un portant l'autre.[14]

Without subordination or privileged explanation the description of what Vincent Berger thinks he sees is presented to the reader as pure fact – even, on this occasion, in the prevailing narrative tense, the past historic. Only with hindsight does the illusion become apparent; only with hindsight do we realize how the objective narrative has been subverted.

Free indirect style and its allies and derivatives occur throughout Malraux's writings with varying degrees of refinement. When used discreetly their effect in terms of increased immediacy is unquestionable; when over-exploited they become banal and restrictive. By his espousing of such devices Malraux demonstrates admirable technical awareness rather than any unique originality. By this brief charting of certain variations in his utilization of them, I hope to have underscored still more heavily the degree to which his commitment to involvement, to *engagement*, as well as moral, political, and spiritual, was necessarily and demonstrably aesthetic. Indeed, it may well be that many of the apparent enigmas of Malraux's intellectual itinerary result only from a lack of understanding in the observer of the degree to which he was preoccupied with his quest for an effective mode of expression, a voice able to inform appropriately his vision of the human condition.

CHAPTER FIVE

On the Comic

la mystification est
éminemment créatrice.
(Malraux, "Du livre," *Catalogue d'éditions
originales et de livres illustrés*)

It seems reasonable to contend that any diachronic consideration of Malraux's comic substance must in some way take as its starting point a concern for the term "farfelu." Commentators have often pointed out the consistency with which the term recurs from the first texts to the last, but it may well be that many have been insensitive to its re-evaluation at different periods in Malraux's itinerary. What I shall attempt to do in the pages that follow, having extracted from Malraux's own etymological indications relating to the word "farfelu" two key reference points, is, quite simply, to monitor and interpret their various reappearances.

An initial, if partial, awareness of Malraux's frame of reference in appropriating the term "farfelu" is provided by Clara Malraux in her account of their early years together:

Déja le mot "farfelu" s'inscrivait dans son vocabulaire: quand je m'enquis de son origine, il me fut répondu que ce mot apparaissait très tôt en français et qu'une racine commune le reliait au *farfallo* – "papillon," de l'italien.[1]

But, undoubtedly the most complete and tempting exegesis comes more directly from Malraux himself during a television interview with Roger Stéphane. There, in answer to a question from his interviewer concerning the source of the word "farfelu," Malraux responds: "Rabelais. Rabelais se sert de l'ancienne étymologie, qui implique les andouilles gonflées, et en même temps est sur la fausse étymologie *farfalla* – 'papillon,' et le mélange, l'andouille à aile de papillon, donne ce farfelu."[2] Malraux seems to perceive in his appropriation of "farfelu" a possible fusion of two specific, but disparate, elements –

"andouilles gonflées" and yet "aile de papillon." It is, then, the
established climate from which the term "farfelu" emerges, and not
merely a deplorable professional need to vivisect, which invites one
to approach Malraux's relationship with the comic through two
distinct, but connected, channels – the curiously grotesque and the
gloriously ephemeral or, in more concrete terms, monsters and
butterflies!

Malraux's first literary text, "Mobilités," touches on diverse
aspects of the elements isolated above:

Une bulle aérienne passe, endormie, les pattes repliées, et se crève à l'une
des pointes du croissant.

Alors, pour l'éclairer – une petite flamme très blanche sort de chacune de
ses extrémités et s'y suspend.[3]

The comparatively incidental evocation of this fragile, but inflated,
ethereal creature, capable of metamorphosis, is followed in *Lunes en
papier* by the chronicle of the strange "aérostats" – balloons which are
transmuted into flowers, then fruits, mushrooms, and eventually into
human caricatures of the seven deadly sins. One year later, in the text
of "Les Hérissons apprivoisés," golden buttons metamorphose into
the eyes of cats, and their aerial escapades recall for the narrator the
flitting of luminous butterflies. Already, it would seem, the cast is
being assembled, although for the moment their play remains
fragmented.

It is, however, with *Royaume-farfelu*, some of which had been
prepared as early as 1920, that butterflies and monsters come together
for the first time, as the narrator, escaping from the scorpions of
Isfahan towards Trebizonde, seeks to buy two sirens for his local
prince in order to prove to him their existence: "Son ministre chrétien
lui dit que les sirènes n'existent pas. Il se trompe. Elles existent en
vérité; un chasseur de papillons, dont j'ai fait mon ami, en a vu."[4] The
implicit association of an affinity for butterflies with a capacity to
perceive beyond the purely logical is one to which we shall return
later.

It should, perhaps, be emphasized that at this stage Malraux's
monsters are in no way terrifying; rather they are uniformly depicted
as quaint, playful, little creatures. One makes the acquaintance of
"diables frisés" and "démons à la queue soyeuse," "diables vol-
tigeants," "démons sympathiques"; one discovers "les jeunes
démons qui venaient de couper leurs cornes en signe d'émancipa-
tion" and "les vieux, couverts de fins tatouages bleus et de rides."[5]
Even the Devil himself is presented as "un être doux et effacé."[6]

What conclusions, then, can be tentatively derived from this *occasional* usage of those elements explicitly present for Malraux in his recoining of the term "farfelu"? Merely, perhaps, that it would be reckless to argue more at this point than that they serve, with other elements, to engender the prevailing atmosphere of the fantastic and the incongruous, always within the imaginary, but scarcely disturbing, confines of the Empire of Death, challengingly designated the "Royaume-farfelu."

In considering these early writings it is important not to forget the literary climate in which they were nurtured, for while that climate developed in the shadow of the holocaust of 1914–18, its primary concerns remained aesthetic. Certainly, from the very beginning, Malraux is at pains to point out that he is indeed seeking to create an autonomous universe, one which is not a stylized version of our own. "Il n'y a aucun symbole dans ce livre…" one reads even before the first page of *Lunes en papier*; rather, the prefatory note goes on to inform the reader, the objects to be invoked thereafter will be recognized as "familiers mais étranges." Clearly, such an imaginary metamorphosis of basically "real" objects into other "real" objects, involving the dissociation and reassociation of facets of reality customarily viewed in a certain *habitual* way, projects a process of redisposition which is transparently cubist in nature. It is thus that the reader encounters in "Les Hérissons apprivoisés":

Les faits dans cette auberge deviennent spécieux … Pourquoi, pendant la nuit, mon beau plumet rouge a-t-il quitté mon casque, et est-il allé se coucher en rond sur le canapé? Les objets jusqu'ici ont été envers moi ce qu'il convenait qu'ils fussent.[7]

Nor is it simply in the fabrication of an independent, imaginary world that the early Malraux is marked by his time. It is also possible to underline the presence of most of that range of devices which characterizes the renewal of the comic idiom, manifest in these same years. Accumulation, repetition, lexical invention, pun, ellipsis, exaggeration, attenuation, paradox – *animation, chosification, décousu, saugrenu*: all are there. But what is apparent in his use of the above is a basic gratuitousness, a genuine *qualité ludique* which will soon disappear from his published writings, as a more urgent awareness of the human condition comes to the fore. There is little doubt that "farfelu" in these formative years conveys no more than a whimsical fantasy on life and death.

Before Indochina the youthful Malraux, as Clara confirms, has not yet really been touched by suffering, let alone death, had not encountered viscerally an extreme situation: "la grande faucheuse, il ne l'avait pas encore rencontrée … son ombre ne s'étendait pas encore sur cette vie débutante."[8] Certainly, in Indochina, after his confrontation with the hostility within raw nature and between men, *both* potentially lethal, there is a decisive hardening and refining of his humour and, thereby, a new identity for those twin facets of the *farfelu* that are our present concern.

Perhaps the transitional stage is best illustrated by an example of an aggressive type of comic device absent from the earlier writings. The text, both Ubuesque pastiche and anti-colonial satire, purports to come from Maurice Cognacq, then Governor of Cochinchina, and appeared as the "Editorial" for the third issue of *L'Indochine enchaînée*:

Après avoir bienveillamment tenté, par tous les moyens, de disqualifier ceux qui ne nous approuvent pas, nous les avons amenés à la conviction qu'ils devaient eux-mêmes demander leur condamnation à mort. Poussés par quelques mauvais démons, ils s'y sont opposés. Nous avons donc prononcé nous-même leur condamnation, avec tout l'intérêt dont nous sommes capable, et les avons fait exécuter bienveillamment. Les excellentes sources d'information, dont nous disposons et que nous censurons nous-même, nous permettent d'affirmer qu'ils se sont repentis après leur mort, et nous admirent aujourd'hui sans réserves.[9]

The change was observed by Nino Frank, who attests that Malraux, an erstwhile "farfelu appliqué," had largely thrust aside incidental humour by the time of Pontigny in late 1926. His participation there was rather characterized by "les questions courtes et nettes, les 'ça va sans dire' ... puis, trop rarement à mon gré, un sursaut d'hilarité, merveilleusement jeune, presque candide."[10]

The comic seems to require the withholding of an emotional commitment – "l'épargne d'une dépense affective" according to Freud, "une anesthésie momentanée du cœur" for Bergson;[11] it elicits primarily a complicity between author and reader at the level of the intellect. As such it is far too restrictive, even distanciating, a mechanism for an author who seeks to express concern, let alone real anguish. Henceforth, apart from occasional humour within the dialogue, in Malraux the comic, drastically reduced, is about to become indistinguishable from the tragic – the amusement of the aesthete will become the rictus of mortal man.

There can be no doubt that one of the most revealing events of the *novelistic* period was the editing out in 1949 of the Rensky episode from the original edition of *Les Conquérants*. It is, of course, the same rigorous self-disciplining of a natural personal penchant which caused Malraux to suppress elsewhere certain Clappique episodes. *Adventurous* mythomania, for the Malraux of this period, was a viable response to man's fate. *Gratuituous* mythomania, no more than occasional playful interference with historical fact, would only tend to dilute the breathless commitment of the definitive major works. It was just such a tendency which typified Rensky, who admits, for example, to buying small ebony elephants in order to "salt" archaeological digs:

j'achète des petits éléphants. Lorsque nous entreprendrons des fouilles, je les mettrai dans les tombeaux que nous refermerons. Cinquante ans plus tard, ceux qui ouvriront de nouveau les cercueils les trouveront au fond, dûment patinés et rongés, et seront intrigués ... J'aime à intriguer ceux qui viendront après moi: sur l'une des tours d'Angkor-Wat, cher ami, j'ai gravé une inscription en langue sanscrite extrêmement obscène, salie avec soin, elle semble très ancienne. Finot la déchiffrera. Il faut scandaliser les hommes austères, un petit peu ...[12]

Perhaps I may, in passing, be permitted to relate a not dissimilar passage from a little-known Malraux text, a preface, written while he was at *La Nouvelle Revue française*, for a rare book catalogue. It takes the form of a dialogue between a bibliophile and a cat.[13] Here is the ending:

Le Bibliophile: Mais toute passion ne fait que créer un besoin que satisfait seule l'illusion de perfection.
Le Chat: Tout cela est vrai: c'est pourquoi il faut devenir faussaire. Ton exemplaire de la *Salome* de Wilde, je l'ornerai d'une dédicace ingénieuse à... à qui? à Lord Queensbury, ton *Corneille*, d'un quatrain autographe à la Marquise. Quelques livres dédiés au citoyen-général Bonaparte sont à souhaiter. Je dessinerai des objets choisis en marge de ton Mallarmé, et les signerai s.m.; nous lirons des articles sur la peinture de Mallarmé, pleins d'aperçus: la mystification est éminemment créatrice.[14]

Incidentally, the degree to which whimsy, specifically here in the form of comic myth-making, was a temptation which Malraux the novelist had *deliberately* to exorcize was borne out for me by the delicious discovery of a friend's copy of the Haakon Chevalier translation of *Le Temps du mépris*, a copy Malraux himself has illustrated with eleven of his drawings. There on the title-page one reads in Malraux's handwriting "illustré de onze dessins originaux par Haakon Chevalier – André Malraux." There is also below the later laconic addendum of M. Chevalier himself – "Pas vrai! – Haakon M. Chevalier."

The second principal period in Malraux's evolution would seem to extend approximately from Indochina to the early post-war years. Certainly during this period one can point to substantial alteration in the frame of reference to be associated with butterfly and monster, as the notion of the *farfelu* becomes inseparable from a confrontation with man's tragic condition.

Perhaps the most challenging appearances of butterflies in the novels are those which see them dancing around a dead, even multilated, human body. They seem to serve as a mocking, natural, counterpart to the futility of human activity: "Kassner s'était bien des fois demandé ce que valait la pensée en face de ses deux cadavres sibériens, au sexe écrasé, des papillons autour du visage."[16] Or, in the wake of Barca's attack on the armoured train the narrator observes: "A côté de lui, Barca, l'épicier du village était mort: l'ombre d'un papillon dansait sur sa figure."[17] In other circumstances scribes have used a dancing butterfly to communicate beauty, mirth, and even conjugal bliss, and Malraux, as demonstrated above, had earlier situated it as an integral, humorous, part of his very literary *farfelu*. Here, however, the reader is bruised by a dimension which transcends the mere corpse and the mere butterfly; for the latter conditions our perception of the former and our very human sensibilities are jarred by the confrontation. An element of levity has now become a device which refines and heightens the tragic sentiment. The *farfelu* is in the process of being revalued.

A similar conclusion could be posited by examining the evolution encountered in Malraux's range of monsters, as the frivolity of that titillating, adoptive, "y" in Malraux's spelling of "dyables" is replaced by the gaping leer of the death mask.

Whether one considers Clappique's face – "une de ces belles gueules avec lesquelles on fait les morts"[18] – as monstrous or not, there is no doubt that his tormented facial approximations of grimacing masks derive from the same agonizing lucidity as Möllberg's monsters in *Les Noyers de l'Altenburg*. Just as in the mask, just as in the monster, just as in the demon, one is dealing with a wilful exteriorization of an aspect of the human soul – for Clappique is studying himself in the mirror:

Il s'approcha encore, le nez touchant presque la glace; il déforma son masque, bouche ouverte, par une grimace de gargouille...

Il transforma son visage, bouche fermée et tirée vers le menton, yeux entrouverts, en samouraï de carnaval. Et aussitôt, comme si l'angoisse, que les paroles ne suffisaient pas à traduire, se fut exprimée directement dans toute sa puissance, il commença à grimacer, se transformant en singe, en idiot, en épouvanté, en type à fluxion, en tous les grotesques que peut exprimer un visage humain.[19]

Möllberg's monsters are, if anything, even more revealing; for although at first glance these have all the endearing fantasy of the early "dyables," they are now primarily characterized by an unpleasant viscosity and a dreadful sadness:

Sur tous les meubles étaient posés d'extraordinaires petits personnages, les uns de glaise, les autres de bronze, qu'il avait pris d'abord pour des fétiches: ils avaient été modelés par Möllberg, qui les appelait ses monstres. Le mot leur convenait mal. C'étaient des animaux imaginaires, pingouins à face de chat, écureuils à nageoires, poissons à tête d'ectoplasme, rapaces à corps de singe: d'un style mou, comme sculptés dans une graisse aux trois-quarts liquéfiée; et tous d'une tristesse saisissante, celle des monstres de Goya qui semblent se souvenir d'avoir été hommes ...[20]

Not surprisingly, it is while reflecting at length on Goya, in an essay of the late 1940s, that Malraux best expresses the bitter significance of a *farfelu* in which the potentially comic serves only to render more poignantly man's plight: "ce ricanement devant la condition humaine ... c'est celui des condamnés. On a de l'esprit dans les préaux qui s'ouvrent sur l'exécution."[21] The gentle chuckle of playful, intellectual complicity has indeed become, provisionally, the universal rictus of death.

The definitive point in this *farfelu* itinerary is reached in *Le Miroir des limbes*, and there, I suspect, the choice of a Buddhist exergual quotation merits attention. But the problem is posed most clearly during Malraux's dialogue with General de Gaulle: " – Mon général, pourquoi faut-il que la vie ait un sens?"[22] Characteristically, Malraux proceeds to provide his own reflective answer, and it is towards the East that he turns for illumination: the Bhagavad Gita becomes Elephanta, becomes Oman, becomes Singapore, as we are focused relentlessly once more onto *butterflies*! Indeed, the fundamental importance of this text is attested by the fact that it is, to my knowledge, the *only* substantial passage to occur in virtually identical form *twice* in *Le Miroir des limbes*.[23] And it is this passage which elucidates the final character of the allusive butterfly.

Its patent mortality – "la vie moyenne d'un papillon dure deux mois"[24] – is decisively offset for Malraux, both by the duration of its tenacious survival as a form of life on this planet – "ils ont deux cent soixante millions d'années"[25] and by its ubiquity – "depuis l'Equateur jusqu'au cap Nord ... presque jusqu'au sommet de l'Himalaya."[26] Obviously, this insistence on the imperturbable continuity of the butterfly's collective existence does invite a meditation on the *relativeness* of human anguish in the ongoing flow of life. And certainly Malraux guides his reader in this direction by recalling: "le texte sacré de l'Inde où les grands papillons, après le combat, viennent se poser sur les guerriers morts et sur les vainqueurs endormis."[27] The development from the dead grocer in *L'Espoir* and the mutilated corpses of *Le Temps du mépris* is dramatic. For now the butterfly is no longer a cavorting mockery of man's absurd fate, but a solemn confirmation of a scheme of things which transcends life *and* death. A rhythm in which men are merely for Malraux "des papillons ... présomptueux."[28]

Elsewhere in *Le Miroir*, too, the butterfly is always associated with the *supra-logical*. Be it the whimsical butterfly on the end of Balkis's nose as she greets Solomon, or the butterfly-shaped stain on the mysterious cloth that the medium, Madame Khodari-Pacha, projects as belonging to Alexander, Malraux himself is in no doubt – "il appartient au sacré."[29]

A similar association with a divine, recast in human terms, is to be discovered in the references to "fétiches" and masks which furnish a common décor for the meditations and conversations of *Le Miroir des limbes*.

For example, the Katchina dolls of the Hopi Indians, costumed, with admirable coherence for my thesis, like "papillons géométriques," are designated by Malraux "divinités du farfelu."[30] Indeed, they have the *particular* function of providing some naïve access to the mystery of the spiritual – "elles permettent aux enfants d'identifier les Esprits."[31] The use of *farfelu*, then, for these fetish dolls is entirely compatible with the argument that this term is now no longer evocative of either the fantastic or the tragic, but is rather related to an image of transcendence within a human perspective. We are faced with precisely the same, atemporal, resonance when Malraux confesses elsewhere "j'aime les musées farfelus, parce qu'ils jouent avec l'éternité."[32]

It is Picasso who crystallizes for Malraux this same idea with regard to the mask, another omnipresent element of the décor of these "limbes." Picasso – "ce farfelu magique ... habité par la métamorphose plus profondément que par la mort"[33] – emphasizes the degree to which the mask is itself magical in that it allows the world an autonomous existence, one no longer subordinate to the concept of an external, absolute, force:

Les masques, ils n'étaient pas des sculptures comme les autres. Pas du tout. Ils étaient des choses magiques ... Mais tous les fétiches, ils servaient à la même chose. Ils étaient des armes. Pour aider les gens à ne plus obéir aux esprits, à devenir indépendants. Des outils. Si nous donnons une forme aux esprits, nous devenons indépendants.[34]

The mask, too, a last metonymical avatar of the monstrous, "appartient au sacré."[35]

It may be appropriate, in conclusion, to sum up the evolution I perceive in the value Malraux attaches, at different points in his writings, to those curious twins – the butterfly and the monster – which have provided the loose structure for this investigation of the *farfelu*. The basic shift is from the primacy of death, couched in contexts that are first playful and then agonized, to the primacy of an always tentatively interrogative transcendence: "l'aléatoire de l'homme précaire"[36] – to invoke Malraux's very last and vital text. Within this grossly simplified framework, the essentially gratuitous, comic, associations of the early writings disappear, as the comic becomes a springboard for deeper entry into the tragic. Finally, both tragic and comic, devoid of any contagion, are relegated to subordinate roles in a vision preoccupied with the question of the sacred.

Malraux, "farfelu numéro un" as he referred to himself privately,[37] has discovered, like Méry, "à l'approche de la mort,"[38] the real significance man must attach to butterflies, has understood, like the aging Picasso, the true meaning of the mask. The smile of the *farfelu* now joins the archaic smile of sculpture[39] in signifying for Malraux that Man has reached into himself and once more made contact with his soul.

CHAPTER SIX

On Tibetan Symbolism

Du haut des couvents aux toits
plats des provinces thibétaines,
le plus beau mystère descend …
(Malraux, *La Tentation de l'Occident*, 18)[1]

In the half-light of a Shanghai bedroom, a man slowly approaches a naked Chinese prostitute. As he lowers himself towards her, his eye glimpses, momentarily, on the wall, a Tibetan painting representing two skeletons locked in an embrace. Fleeting, but so provocative, this curious little scene taken from Malraux's *La Condition humaine* seems to have gone largely unnoticed by critics and has never elicited to my knowledge an analysis of any depth. At best, readers point cursorily to the passage's prophetically morbid quality, the lack of genuine contact, the very mortal reality that the flesh momentarily couches. And yet it happens to occur at a most meaningful point in the novel – immediately prior to the accelerated dénouement which commences with Tchen's suicidal attack on Chang-Kai-Chek – and has been carefully prepared by the preceding philosophical discussion between Ferral and Gisors which conceptualizes erotic experience. Nor, moreover, is this likely to be a chance reference, for Malraux's considerable awareness of Asian art and its overtones was already well established by 1933 when the novel first appeared.[2] It would seem worthwhile, therefore, without recklessly positing any iconographical intentionality on the part of the author, at least to reflect more speculatively than has been attempted hitherto on the potential areas of significance of a moment which Malraux himself presents thus:

Il [Ferral] comprenait maintenant ce que Gisors n'avait que soupçonné: oui, sa volonté de puissance n'atteignait jamais son objet, ne vivait que de le renouveler; mais n'eût-il de sa vie possédé une seule femme, il avait possédé, il possèderait à travers cette Chinoise qui l'attendait, la seule chose dont il fût avide: lui-même. Il lui fallait les yeux des autres pour se voir, les sens d'une autre pour se sentir. Il regarda la peinture thibétaine: sur un monde décoloré où erraient des voyageurs, deux squelettes exactement semblables s'étreignaient en transe.

Il s'approcha de la femme.[3]

Who are these skeletons? Why are they embracing? What is the importance of their identical forms? What is the impact of the trance they are experiencing? What does the background mean? What relationship do they have to the encounter about to take place below? These are just some of the questions which must surely be considered if we are to enter fully into Malraux's vision of man.

A suitable departure point in seeking some tentative answers would be to note that, in the Lamaist pantheon, intertwined skeletons are usually associated with Yama, the Buddhist Pluto or God of Death;[4] indeed, some scholars maintain that in many instances they are actually emanations of Yama himself. Certainly, the stories which surround Yama project most forcefully an intriguingly Malrucian aura of death, dominance, menace, and sexuality. In his most common avatar, Yama is portrayed in threatening, bull-headed form, bearing in the right hand a skull-topped club, and in the left a snare or skull cap filled with blood. His attribute, the blue-coloured bull on which he is standing, is itself kneeling on a female body which it is either crushing or penetrating sexually. Not infrequently, Yama himself is depicted with penis erect.[5]

Perhaps more inviting, and certainly more profoundly instructive, is the main legend relating to Yama, one which seems to propose Death, not as a total negative, but rather in the guise of a challenge or interrogative, as an experience which must in some way be contested. It would, of course, be banal to stress the aptness of this to Malraux's vision of the human condition.

There is no doubt that in the Tibetan scheme of things the God of Death is far from being an emphatic Absolute, for he undergoes the same torments as more mortal beings in order to expiate his own particular sins. By some fundamental contradiction, he is both Lord over Death and a finite being. Indeed, to followers of the Lamaist faith, Death appears to be conquerable, or such would seem to be the conclusion to be drawn from the most prevalent legend.[6] According to the story, a holy man once withdrew from the world to meditate in a cave for fifty years, so that he would be worthy to enter the blessed state of Nirvana. On the night before his fifty-year vigil was to end, two thieves entered his retreat with a stolen bull, which they proceeded to kill by cutting off its head. Subsequently discovering the presence of the aged ascetic, the robbers decided to get rid of him because he was a witness to their crime. In despair the hermit begged them to spare his life, explaining that if he were killed before the allotted time he would lose the entire benefit of his fifty years' devotion, and would no longer enter Nirvana. But the thieves refused to heed him and cut off his head. Thereupon, his body assumed the ferocious form of Yama and, setting the bull's head upon his own headless shoulders, he proceeded to kill the two murderers, drinking their blood from cups made of their skulls. His fury at being deprived of immense spiritual fulfilment undiminished, he then threatened to depopulate the whole of Tibet. In their plight, the Tibetans appealed to their tutelary deity, Manjusri, to protect them from this formidable enemy, and Manjusri, in the form of Yamantaka ("he who conquers death"), took up their cause. In the awesome struggle which ensued, Yamantaka was ultimately victorious and the God of Death defeated.

Although we have up to this point been considering Yama himself as a possible key to the intertwined skeletons in Malraux's image, most iconographers would probably prefer to see in them the standard representation of the Citipati.[7] The Citipati were not, in fact, themselves gods, but were, as suggested earlier, important acolytes in the suite of Yama. However, on occasion, legend does seem to have merged inextricably the stories that once, perhaps, distinguished divinity and adherent. Certainly, there is a close similarity between the narrative concerning Yama recounted above and a northern Buddhist tale explaining the origin of the Citipati. According to the prevalent account of that tale, the latter were in a former existence two holy men who were once lost in such deep meditation that they did not notice that a thief had cut off their heads and thrown them in the dust. Since that time they have been linked by their ferocious enmity for the assassin and are eternally in quest of vengeance and satisfaction.[8]

It is apparent that the two legends overlap in a common frame of reference which encompasses violence, death, the frustration of an almost transcendental state and, most significantly for our present loose critical association, a continuing rejection of any passivity in the face of Death.

Symptomatically, these same ingredients are also to be discovered perpetuated in the Tibetan "Mystery Play," performed annually at monasteries throughout the Himalayan region, and described by L.A. Waddell in his authoritative work on Lamaism.[9] In these productions which fuse Bon and Buddhist traditions, the principals include Yama and his minions – notably, among the latter, skeletal figures evocative of the Citipati. It is worth remarking in passing on that particular moment of the ceremonial play when a holy man blesses a goblet of water by laying his hands on it and intoning a prayer. This pious act cows the shrieking ghouls who creep out of the arena leaving no sound but the sweet chant of the holy choir. However, the power of the exorcism is short-lived, for the spectres soon return. Once again, the conclusion that the repetition of this scene within the play imposes is one of continual and heroic striving in a desperate conflict.

Although the recurrent elements in the above descriptions do establish the relevance of a certain prevailing atmosphere, closer investigation of the usual plastic representation of the figures in question offers a still more focused illumination of Malraux's text.

Against a background of stylized flames, and often surrounded by countless *dakini* (i.e., "lesser" divinities), the Citipati appear on Tibetan paintings as identical skeletal forms with arms and legs interlaced in some sort of strange embrace – perhaps born of eroticism, perhaps of dance, perhaps of mutual restraint. Both forms brandish a club-like sceptre topped with a skull, and may carry a skull cup or other sacred object. The grimaces on their fleshless faces seem to vacillate enigmatically between a smile of joy from some unrevealed awareness and the agony of unrelenting rictus.[10]

What then of Malraux? Let us now superimpose this "fuller" image onto his more succinct version cited above.

First, the shadowy infernal background ("monde décoloré") fleetingly multiplies through its scattered travellers those who attend or bear witness to the state of the Citipati, multiplies thus indefinitely, by proxy, the human protagonists about to embrace on the bed below. In this way Ferral's situation is depersonalized and becomes general, for our investigation suggests that the background figures are of the same species as those in the foreground – both are *dakini*, endowed with great power but less than divine in the fullest sense of the word; they are heroic but mortal. Second, the trance-like condition ("en transe") of the two skeletons alluded to by Malraux[11] not only reinvokes the state of deep meditation already discovered in the legendary sources from which the Citipati emerge, it also reaffirms that alienation of lucidity so often characteristic of both erotic activity and dance, where rhythmic physical patterns "transport" the practicant.

However, among the detail Malraux has furnished, there is no doubt that it is the total similarity of the two skeletons ("exactement semblables") which is most conducive to fruitful reflection. This specific emphasis on identical form would seem to override the general novelistic context which, in offering them as a backcloth to Ferral and the courtesan, invites us at first glance to consider the skeletons as male and female. Certainly, in their paintings of the Citipati, the Tibetan artists make no evident anatomical distinction, and iconographers customarily interpret the two figures as the *Sakta* and the *Sakti*, twin aspects of a single nature.[12] In aesthetic terms, we appear to be faced with a sort of skeletal *mise en abyme*, as ultimately self-reflexive in quality as the "mirror" paintings of Velazquez, Quetzys, and Memling. Nor does the reference within the passage to an embrace ("étreinte") justify a reading that assumes the heterosexual, for the word and its derivatives appear primarily in Malraux in association with gestures of virile fraternity. Even in the explicit context of a man-woman relationship, Malraux tends deliberately to blur the distinct physical differences which make the act, at least potentially, productive. Many critics, such as Bataille, do choose to accent the reproductive aspects of the erotic embrace: "s'il est vrai que l'érotisme se définit par l'indépendance de la jouissance érotique et de la reproduction comme fin, le sens fondamental de la reproduction n'en est pas moins la clé de l'érotisme."[13]

However, in Malraux's writings, the act of embracing seems to be totally removed from any overtones of this sort. Indeed, one could even contend that in a Malraux novel an embrace, erotic or otherwise, is essentially homosexual, or perhaps asexual. There is no doubt that in his writings prior to *La Condition humaine*, Malraux already suggested that eroticism in purely sexual terms was a fruitless experience, for any satisfactions that it might achieve were provisional. As I indicated in an earlier chapter, in *Les Conquérants* Garine finds only fleeting release in brief therapeutic interludes: "Lorsqu'on est ici depuis un certain temps ... les Chinoises énervent beaucoup, tu verras. Alors pour s'occuper en paix de choses sérieuses, le mieux est de coucher avec elles et n'y plus penser."[14]

And in *La Voie royale*, Perken, who prefigures Ferral in so many ways, is frustrated in his desire to leave a scar on the world through which he passes, but does make a striking and significantly new appraisal of the erotic experience: "L'essentiel est de *ne pas connaître* la partenaire. Qu'elle soit l'autre sexe."[15] It is this reduction of the role of the *specific* partner, here still female, which is later taken up and developed by Ferral, who recognizes that "En somme il ne couchait jamais qu'avec lui-même."[16] Nor, in this age of equality, it should be noted, is this projection of the erotic experience as self-directed confined to the male of the species, as Malraux's sympathetic discussion of Constance's activities in his article on Lawrence's *Lady Chatterley's Lover* confirms:

il fallait que les rapports entre elle et son nouvel amant fussent impersonnels, il fallait qu'elle devînt sa maîtresse avant de savoir *qui* il est, *avant du lui avoir parlé*. De quoi a-t-elle besoin? De se révéler à elle-même à l'aide de sa propre sexualité. Peu importe le moyen de cet éveil. Que Mellors se réduise d'abord à un sexe adroit et anonyme: qu'il ne soit, à aucun titre, le séducteur; le vrai dialogue est entre Lady Chatterley et elle-même.[17]

I have already examined in some detail in chapter 3 the erotic encounter between Ferral and Valérie which immediately precedes the allusion to the Tibetan painting. There is no doubt that it is the anguished frustration which that experience generates in Ferral that causes him to seek relief in still another body. And yet the irony is clear: for Ferral's inability to attain any supreme fulfilment or real self-affirmation in his relationship with Valérie is not a function of their particular characters or idiosyncrasies, but rather a testimony to the inadequacy of *all* erotic experience to provide *any* Absolute. Ferral is thus doomed inevitably to rediscover in each fleeting fleshly gratification, including his latest Chinese courtesan, the same desperate void. For he will persevere – the erotic will remain as a perpetual invitation and challenge to a now Godless man, however ultimately ineffectual any effort is destined to be.

It is this message, therefore, which is both encapsulated and expanded in the image of the intertwined skeletons over Ferral's bed – the thrust of their iconographic energy being twofold. First, as I have suggested, they serve to fix plastically by their identical appearances the fundamentally impersonal and asexual quality of true eroticism; but more importantly, they also encourage by their evident association with Death an exegesis which establishes the erotic act as among the most significant of mortal experiences. In this way, *la petite mort*, as it is appositely known, becomes *the* symbol of our human condition, in a life lived out painfully – and yet enquiringly, even wilfully, claims Malraux – under the dreadful spectre of Death. Gisors, as so often, seems to speak for his creator when he suggests:

Peut-être l'amour est-il surtout le moyen qu'emploie l'Occidental pour s'affranchir de sa condition d'homme ... La maladie chimérique, dont la volonté de puissance n'est que la justification intellectuelle, c'est la volonté de déité: tout homme rêve d'être dieu.[18]

Man seeking to become Manjusri. And at almost the same period, having traced in his commentary on *Lady Chatterley's Lover* evolving attitudes through the centuries, Malraux states still more clearly, in his own voice, this vital role of eroticism in the twentieth century as an experiential circumstance by which to affirm oneself fully, to achieve an intensity close to that once attributed to God:

d'en faire le moyen de notre propre révélation ... il s'agit d'être homme – le plus possible. C'est à dire de faire de notre conscience érotique, dans ce qu'elle a de plus viril, le système de références de notre vie.[19]

It will have been apparent from much of the preceding conjecture that the question of intentionality holds no interest here, in a few pages that, perhaps somewhat vicariously, are determined to be reflective and interrogative rather than exhaustive or affirmative. But, in conclusion, I would contend with some confidence that that fugitive allusion to an unidentified Tibetan *thanka* with which this chapter concerns itself, evoking as it does not only sexuality, frustration, solitude, and joy, but above all the dreadful enigma of death – the whole stylized and etherealized to the level of a metaphysical question mark – may well be the most profound symbol of Man to be found anywhere in Malraux's writings.

CHAPTER SEVEN

On the Renunciation of the Novel

L'histoire de la technique du récit suit
essentiellement la recherche d'une
troisième dimension, de ce qui dans le
roman échappe au récit, de ce qui permet
non de raconter, mais de représenter,
de rendre présent. (Malraux, "N'était-ce donc
que cela?")[1]

As already observed in earlier chapters, the emphatic tone of the above exergual statement is repeated on other occasions by Malraux, as he insists on the vital importance for him of achieving immediacy in a novel:

On peut analyser la mise en scène d'un grand romancier. Que son objet soit le récit de faits, la peinture ou l'analyse de caractères, voire une interrogation sur le sens de la vie; que son talent tende à une prolifération, comme celui de Proust, ou à une cristallisation, comme celui de Hemingway, il est amené à raconter – c'est-à-dire à rendre présent.[2]

Indeed, right from the very beginning of his own novelistic career the essence of his narrative technique was precisely that – "*rendre présent.*" Malraux attempted to re-create the action and atmosphere of his story around the reader; the aesthetic problem that he sought to resolve is that of the painter who attempts a three-dimensional effect with two-dimensional means. It is not particularly original to assert that to a certain extent every art tends towards that point which seems most distant from its fundamental nature: the artist seeks relief, even infinity, on a canvas within a restricting frame; the sculptor may attempt to animate, to humanize an inert block of stone; the film director has increasingly sought to interiorize the stubbornly objective eye of the camera. Malraux in each of his novels wanted to reveal to his reader a vision of the world that was real and immediately present, and not a literary construct, subordinated by the author, and at a recognizable, even comfortable, distance from the reader.

The various devices of which Malraux made use in this quest for immediacy are too numerous to catalogue in detail here, but there are those which demand mention by the frequency with which they reappear. Some of these techniques are intended to suppress the distance which often exists between the action of the story and the reader: the use of the present tense eliminates temporal distance; the use of a first person narrator lessens the spatial distance between the action and the recounting by making the narrator an eyewitness; free indirect style allows the reader to "receive" a character's thoughts directly, without intellectualization and subordination by the author. Other devices attempt to concretize and to underline some idea or action – to this effect it is the figurative language which is most developed. By his use of imagery Malraux emphasizes what he is describing and gives physical substance to abstract notions. In addition, with the aid of techniques which are sometimes claimed as being specifically cinematographic, Malraux "visualized" his narrative and invested it, at times, almost with the plastic quality of film.

The international standing of André Malraux, novelist, is such that it would seem reasonable to believe that these techniques had been largely successful and convincing; however, for Malraux himself, the value of his novels as narrative vehicles, indeed the value of any novel, would seem to be in some doubt.

There appeared in 1971 in *French Studies* a review of Carduner's admirable book on Malraux's style.[3] But, having recognized the great merit of the study, the reviewer went on to regret that "The writer's [Carduner's] analytical method underlines the *constant* features of Malraux's narrative technique rather than its evolution." A valid reservation perhaps, for so striking is this evolution that it can provide the key to an extremely plausible aesthetic solution to Malraux's renunciation of the novel. It is certainly possible to trace a definite stylistic progression from the beginning of Malraux's career as a novelist to its abrupt termination, when, utterly disillusioned with literary fiction, he abandoned the genre irrevocably: "Comme technique narrative l'écriture n'existe pas."[4] The novels were in the creative life of André Malraux no more than a phase in a long and fragmented quest for a suitable means of self-expression. Malraux renounced his career as a novelist after the appearance in 1943 of *Les Noyers de l'Altenburg*, and, according to Roger Stéphane in an account of a conversation with him, had in 1944 the intention of continuing with the career of film director which he had broached a few years earlier with *Sierra de Teruel*. Thus Malraux's desire to forge an effective narrative technique seemed to be about to continue even after the period of the novels, for as we shall see, having modified his literary equipment on several occasions, without ultimate satisfaction, he intended to turn more definitely towards the cinema.

The decisive technique in Malraux's first novel, *Les Conquérants*, is in fact double: the structural combination of the systematic use of the present tense and a first person narrator. The value of the present tense in a narrative is not difficult to discern: it allows the dramatic presentation of otherwise distant events,[5] and the reader can thus better participate in the imaginative experience of the writer. But it is not only the temporal distance between the reader and the events which is suppressed, for the spatial distance, too, is bridged by the device of a first person narrator with whom the reader can identify. For this first person as a character does not really exist: his function is purely to serve as the representative of the reader in the story; he is the sensorial mass by which the reader receives the story. On these two techniques, therefore, was founded Malraux's initial attempt to seize the reader from his nineteenth-century armchair and plunge him into the action.

We have already investigated in an earlier chapter Malraux's use of the present tense in this and subsequent novels, and contended that the unbroken utilization in this particular novel dilutes any dramatic potential. Similarly with the first person narrator; although it does allow some striking effects of immediacy as the reader becomes a virtual participant by identification, it too tends to lose its effectiveness by over-exploitation. It is also certain that a narrative written entirely in the first person does pose certain structural problems, and imposes on the novel the limitations of *I*.

In *Les Conquérants* the presence of the narrator during the vital confrontation between Garine and Tcheng-Dai would be unnatural since the narrator's rank could in no way sanction this, for despite his friendship with Garine, which certainly gives him an added prestige, his actual functions remain modest. Thus Malraux had to find another means by which to relate the details of this crucial interview, and this he contrived by presenting in a subsequent scene a transcript of that conversation between Garine and Tcheng-Dai. Other allied problems of consistency faced Malraux, for unless this first person was omniscient his knowledge was necessarily limited, and therefore certain details of Garine's past life had to be presented in the form of unwieldy reported conversations.

Nevertheless one cannot deny the considerable effect of the use of the first person. The increase in immediacy which one receives from an eyewitness is a basic fact of life, but Malraux goes much further, and, by a total fidelity to the angle of his story, manages to augment even more the efficacy of the technique. On several occasions, for example, the narrator enters a room while a conversation is in progress in the interior, and with him the reader steps *in medias res* and must, with him, discover the course of the conversation:

Lorsque je redescends au premier étage une rumeur de paroles et des bruits d'armes viennent, par les fenêtres, de la rue nocturne ...

Garine, assis derrière son bureau, mange une longue flûte de pain grillé qui craque entre ses dents, et parle au général Gallen qui l'écoute en marchant à travers la pièce.

–... Je ne peux pas donner dès maintenant des conclusions. Mais d'après les quelques rapports que j'ai déjà reçus, je peux affirmer ceci: il y a partout des îlots de résistance; il y a dans la ville la possibilité d'une nouvelle tentative semblable à celle de Tang.

–Il est pris, Tang?

–Non.

–Mort?

–Je ne sais pas encore. Mais aujourd'hui c'est Tang, deman ce sera un autre. L'argent de l'Angleterre est toujours là, et l'Intelligence Service aussi. On lutte ou on ne lutte pas. Mais...

Il se lève, souffle sur le bureau, secoue ses vêtements pour en chasser les miettes de pain, va au coffre fort, l'ouvre et en tire un tract qu'il donne à Gallen.

–... voici l'essentiel.

–Hein! cette vieille crapule!

–Non, il ignore certainement l'existence de ces tracts.

Je regarde par-dessus l'épaule de Gallen: le tract annonce la constitution d'un nouveau gouvernement dont la présidence aurait été offerte à Tcheng-Dai.[6]

During this passage the narrator-reader gathers little by little the subject under discussion. The allusions to "conclusions" and "tentative" become clear only when *we* read the tract. Thus, despite the occasionally tortuous paths into which the author is led by the choice of a first person narrator, Malraux does manage to make use of the apparent limitations in order to thrust the reader into the events. There is another instance of this in the exactitude with which Malraux transposes a telephone call – the words are those of Garine:

Encore la sonnerie du téléphone intérieur.

–.......

Mais quels émeutiers, bon sang!

–.......

Tu devrais le savoir.

–.......

Oui enfin, comment sont-ils arrivés?

–.......

Plusieurs banques? Bon. Laisse-les attaquer. Il raccroche et quitte la pièce.[7]

The spaces which replace the replies of the person at the other end of the line are utterly faithful to reality, for clearly the narrator can only hear the voice of Garine. These almost insignificant details, by their fidelity and credibility, contribute a great deal to the overall effect of "being present."

Malraux's first novel, Les Conquérants, reveals quite unequivocally the aesthetic considerations which were to preoccupy him as a novelist. This initial attempt to resolve the limitations of narrative, although crude by comparison with the use of similar techniques in later works, does indicate the writer's wish for a narrative form capable of placing the reader in the action and of eliminating conventional literary distance.

Although after Les Conquérants the first person narrative is rejected until its modified reappearance in Malraux's last novel, its natural literary prolongation, free indirect style, does appear in the second novel, La Voie royale. But it remains at this point embryonic and only emerges subsequently as a full and major technique. For the moment, while continuing to seek immediacy, Malraux chooses to explore a very different stylistic arena.

The general stylistic substance of La Voie royale can perhaps loosely be called figurative,[8] which is to say that, whereas in the preceding novel the author's principal device was structural, now Malraux attempts to enclose the reader in a coherent network of symbol and comparison. This does not imply mystification, for, despite those esoterics who may wish to obscure, the fundamental value of metaphor is to clarify.

It is through the imagery in this second novel that Malraux seeks to translate and emphasize the struggle of man and fate, the battle which begins anew each day that Claude and Perken penetrate further into the combined horror of the forest and its inhuman inhabitants. The adventurer-hero, Perken, is the personification of Will – "je veux laisser une cicatrice sur cette carte" – and throughout the novel the reader follows his efforts to affront the "universelle désagrégation."[9]

In this work all the elements which oppose the progress of the two men are assimilated by imagery to the treacherous subhuman quality of the forest.

The chapter where Malraux relates the incident between Perken and the Moïs is full of examples where the native warriors are described in insect terms, and are thus presented as an integral part of the active frustration that characterizes the forest:

Les Moïs sortaient sans qu'il vît par où, se coulaient dans le sentier avec leurs gestes précis de guêpes, avec leurs armes de mantes.

Ils avançaient en fourmis, toujours le long de la ligne mystérieuse, vers la gauche.

Il [Perken] dépendait totalement de cet être, de ses pensées de larve.

... la rumeur passait sur l'assemblée presque toute perdue dans l'ombre comme un bruissement d'insectes.[10]

As Carduner states so clearly, the forest and its inhabitants are a manifestation of the hostility and immensity against which man strives to assert himself. The certainty of the ultimate defeat of man is symbolized at the beginning of the novel when Perken, aboard a ship passing slowly along the Sumatran coast, experiences a feeling of apprehension:

Il ne pouvait délivrer son regard des taches dans lesquelles se perdaient les plantes. Se frayer un chemin à travers une semblable végétation? D'autres l'avaient fait, il pourrait donc le faire. A cette affirmation inquiète, le ciel bas et l'inextricable tissu des feuilles criblées d'insectes opposaient leur affirmation silencieuse.[11]

This feeling, confirmed by the fate of Grabot, a prefiguration of Perken's own, attests to the greatness of man, who, while recognizing the tragic certainty of his fate, refuses to accept in passivity.

In *La Voie royale* it is by the frequency and vividness of his figurative language that Malraux seeks to translate his thought and vision. Whereas in *Les Conquérants* the structural devices were intended to render the action – and therefore, indirectly, the thought – more immediate, in the second novel it is chiefly by virtue of an extensive interweaving of dramatic symbols, which seek to represent in physical form the human condition, that the reader is drawn into the book. The insistent, almost claustrophobic effect that results from the denseness of the imagery associated with the forest would seem to be a specifically literary attempt to reproduce the sensations of Perken and Claude, and to associate the reader directly with the novelistic world and, thereby, with the author's ongoing interrogation of his own.

In *La Condition humaine*, considered by many to be Malraux's best novel, through a tempered combination of those techniques which had earlier appeared in either massive or minimal quantities, the author has forged a highly effective style. He continues to reject the somewhat clumsy first person narrative, but makes frequent use of the closely associated free indirect style. Nearly every major character is revealed to the reader in this way, by permitting direct access to their thoughts. The effect, as we have seen in chapter 4, is a reduction of the spatio-temporal distance between reader and protagonist. It is a technique which, distributed throughout the work, causes us to see the action through the eyes of *a certain* character, and requires us to adopt momentarily *a certain* point of view, reducing in this way the obvious intervention of the author.

Although, as the title suggests, there is a great deal of symbolism in *La Condition humaine*, Malraux does not attempt the same extreme density which was observed in *La Voie royale*. A recurrent symbol in *La Condition humaine* is the strident blast of a horn or siren. Such sounds are, at this stage, more than just a desire for realism prompted by a growing interest in the emergent cinema, for they constitute an attempt to present an abstract notion to the reader in auditive form, and therefore to render it more apparent, and even insistent. From the first pages of the novel these sounds reveal to Tchen a world outside his own particular drama. At the very moment when he is going to kill the sleeping man we read:

Quatre ou cinq klaxons grincèrent à la fois. Découvert? Combattre, combattre des ennemis qui se défendent, des ennemis éveillés, quelle délivrance!

Le vague de vacarme retomba: quelque embarras de voitures (il y avait encore des embarras de voitures, là-bas dans le monde des hommes...).[12]

As soon as he hears this sound Tchen (and the reader) becomes aware of his isolation. This world of death in which he is so involved is *his* world, and we only become aware of another, material, outside world when it imposes itself harshly. The scream of the sirens immediately after the murder bears witness yet more forcefully to this separateness which is for the author a fundamental aspect of the human condition. Dramatically the most effective of these sounds is that heard by the prisoners awaiting execution in the courtyard. The periodic blast of the locomotive announces elliptically that yet another prisoner has been burnt alive. Confronted with the very sound of death, the alienation of the prisoners is complete.

Although their significance clearly transcends mere realism, this frequent use of sounds, for the first time in Malraux's work, was probably suggested by the development of sound in the cinema. Such an assumption would seem to be confirmed by the appearance in this novel of several techniques which are closely associated with the cinema and which are a vital new departure in the evolution of Malraux's novelistic style.

In her book *L'Age du roman américain*, Claude-Edmonde Magny made the important observation that "Notre sensibilité collective a été profondément modifiée sans que nous y prenions garde par le cinéma."[13] She suggested that we no longer perceive the world in the same way as fifty years ago; in particular we are accustomed to *seeing* and *hearing* stories simultaneously. To satisfy our altered sensibility literature must necessarily adapt. It was this need to revitalize the novel which had been the mainspring of Malraux's earlier attempts, and it is not surprising that in this new, vivid, audiovisual medium he should find fresh means to *rendre présent*.

One of the most effective cinematographic techniques which appears in *La Condition humaine* is the use of lighting to isolate and accentuate certain objects or characteristics. On the first page of the novel, when Tchen stands at the side of the sleeping man, we read: "La seule lumière venait du building voisin; un grand rectangle d'électricité pâle, coupé par les barreaux de la fenêtre dont l'un rayait le lit juste au-dessous du pied comme pour en accentuer le volume et la vie."[14] The light, and what is virtually a literary close-up, underlines the physical presence of the foot, and emphasizes the life which the foot symbolizes, without attaching it to any individual – the identity of the owner of the foot is clearly of no importance.

Often an effect of lighting permits the writer to indicate specific physical characteristics which may well have psychological overtones, and nearly all the characters of *La Condition humaine* appear under a lamp, or in front of a streetlight, at some moment.[15]

However, the most purely cinematographic description in *La Condition humaine*, and the one which shows best Malraux's astonishing cinematic vision, occurs at the moment when Katow enters the room of a Communist combat group:

Dix minutes après avoir quitté Kyo, Katow, ayant traversé des couloirs, dépassé des guichets, était arrivé à une pièce blanche, nue, bien éclairée par des lampes-tempête. Pas de fenêtre. Sous le bras du Chinois qui lui ouvrit la porte, cinq têtes penchées sur la table mais le regard sur lui, sur la haute silhouette connue de tous les groupes de choc.[16]

The total whiteness of the room provides a stark background against which the "têtes penchées" seem to prefigure the eventual humiliation of the Communists. But what confirms that Malraux is visualizing this scene with the eye of a *cinéaste* rather than a novelist, or even a dramatist, is the peculiar angle of the shot. Katow, and the reader, see "sous le bras du Chinois"! This combination of lighting, symbolism, and angle is almost pure visual cinema.[17]

It would seem at this stage in his artistic development that Malraux felt himself equipped to produce the narrative chef d'oeuvre which appeared to be the target of his novelistic development – and it is precisely that which, as the preface intimates, he attempted in *Le Temps du mépris.* "L'homme, la foule, les éléments, la femme et le destin" were to provide the *fond*, and the *forme* was to be composed of all those techniques which had been previously tested and tempered in the foregoing novels. But the result is a turnip![18]

The truth is that *Le Temps du mépris*, despite the extreme subtlety of many of the devices which bear witness to an exceptional artistic skill, does not live. It lacks the conviction and solidity of those novels which Malraux had, in part, lived himself. It is a novel of little substance encased in a fascinating, perhaps too brilliant, shell. In what was probably an attempt to simplify and alleviate the structure of this work after the criticism of "obscurité"[19] which had followed the appearance of *La Condition humaine*, Malraux returns in *Le Temps du mépris* to the single point of view of linear narrative such as was found in his earlier novels. He makes extensive use of free indirect style to maintain this point of view and to reproduce forcefully for the reader Kassner's anguish. He seeks to combine the clarity of consistent angle with the immediacy of thoughts directly perceived. But he goes too far,[20] and commits the error of over-interiorizing the story, of reducing it to that "élucidation de l'individu" which he rejects elsewhere.[21] Mental turmoil and its direct revelation are always present in Malraux's novels, but to comment on the action not to replace it. Here the action which Malraux depicts so well in his other novels is pared to a minimum, and the majority of the work is nothing more than a revelation of the partially controlled madness of the protagonist, whose particular psychology is in no way capable of arousing the same reactions as the vigorous complexity and universality of a novel like *La Condition humaine*. In his wish to purify and perfect his fiction, Malraux deprives it of its breath of life.

The failure of this novel was a major disappointment to the author, and it is scarcely surprising that it should be from this same year that remarks such as the following began to multiply: "à l'art qui reposait sur la métaphore se substitue l'art que repose sur l'ellipse [le cinéma]."[22] It is clear that Malraux, from the end of 1935, began to entertain serious doubts about the value of the novel as a means of narrative expression, and glimpsed already in the cinema its possible replacement.

Nevertheless, it is in his next work that Malraux achieves for some his finest novel, *L'Espoir*; for in the Spanish Civil War he finds and lives a subject which is highly suited to his dramatic, elliptic style. All those techniques which had contributed to the dominant aesthetic characteristic of immediacy in the preceding novels appear here, in refined form, to produce the chef d'oeuvre that *Le Temps du mépris* had failed to be.

First, the present tense, which in *Les Conquérants* had been only partially effective, limited both by its very nature and by over-use, appears with great discretion in *L'Espoir*.[23] It is used only to heighten the drama or poignancy of the most critical moments of the story, and the contrast with the narrative preterite tense is such that the increase in immediacy is striking.

Free indirect style, too, is used sparingly, but effectively. One passage, of particular power, occurs when Manuel is watching the enemy tanks advance and is beginning to become anxious:

Manuel reprit ses jumelles. Quelques hommes de son extrême gauche couraient vers les tanks fascistes, qui ne semblaient pas tirer car aucun des hommes ne tombait. Mais – Manuel tournait la molette des jumelles, délayait encore le paysage, le précisait à nouveau derrière la pluie – ils avaient les bras en l'air. Ils passaient à l'ennemi.[24]

Here, we are allowed no general view of what takes place. We perceive only through the blurred field-glasses of Manuel, or more precisely we are only given his vision, and we are as uncertain as he is. Free indirect style, a literary device dating back to the earliest French texts, finds itself here endowed with an almost cinematographic power of illusion, for the filmic device of limiting a spectator's field of vision to that of a character is widespread.[25] However, the question of cinematographic content in *L'Espoir* is not in doubt;[26] indeed in the same year as the book was published, 1937, Malraux was already making a film along similar lines.

In *L'Espoir* imagery and symbolism have continued to be reduced, and, under the growing influence of the cinema, the meaningful sounds of *La Condition humaine* would seem to have become a vast sound track of noises, cries, and songs – the holocaust of the Civil War which is insistently present for the reader. A comparison of the following passage, where Puig is watching and listening to his comrades' efforts to reduce an enemy gun to silence, with the brief allusions to sirens in *La Condition humaine* would bring out this development:

Derrière lui, dans un hurlement haletant de trompes et de klaxons, deux Cadillac arrivaient avec les zigzags balayés des films de gangsters. La première, conduite par le chauve aux petites moustaches, dévala dans le feu convergent des fusils et de la mitrailleuse, sous les obus qui passaient trop haut. Fonçant entre les deux canons, elle rejeta les soldats comme un chasse-neige, et alla s'écraser sur le mur à côté du porche du canon de 37. Le 37 continuait à tirer contre la seconde auto qui fonçait entre les deux canons, son klaxon hurlant, et s'engouffra sous le porche à 120 à l'heure. Le 37 cessa se tirer. De toutes les rues les ouvriers regardaient le trou noir du porche, dans le silence sans klaxon.[27]

The many techniques of a cinematographic nature which are to be found in *L'Espoir*, and which attest to the constancy of Malraux's preoccupations with immediacy, have been fully investigated and detailed by Carduner, and I shall only mention one passage here which again reveals that remarkable sense of composition which was observed in *La Condition humaine*. At the moment when the dynamiters are awaiting the tanks, Malraux describes a scene where Gonzales, a dynamiter, at ground level, sees two ants, dominant by their proximity, while in the background a tank is approaching:

Gonzalez s'allonge. Le tank est à quatre cents mètres, et il ne le voit pas sur les herbes en silhouettes devant ses yeux ... déjà les fourmis s'y baladent ... Derrière deux fourmis très occupées arrive de toute sa vitesse la tache grondante et secouée du tank oblique.[28]

The extent of the influence of the cinema in *L'Espoir*, together with Malraux's professed disillusionment with his preceding novel, and his later confession of extreme mistrust of the novel as a worthwhile narrative form, would seem to suggest that this Spanish experience was destined for the screen from an early date, and would also indicate an imminent abandonment of narrative fiction.

The last of Malraux's novels, *Les Noyers de l'Altenburg*, is very unsatisfactory from an artistic point of view. Although it occasionally manifests similar techniques to those which had been used so felicitously in *L'Espoir*, and flirts with others as yet unformed, there is no real coherence between expression and content. The long central portion of the book, the colloquium, devoted to a discussion of the author's historico-cultural ideas, could almost be an essay, and it certainly reveals the future *literary* direction that Malraux will take, at least for the following quarter of a century.

Malraux's *narrative* direction would seem to be confirmed shortly after the appearance of *Les Noyers de l'Altenburg* in a published conversation with Roger Stéphane: "Nous descendons dîner. Il [Malraux] m'annonce son intention de faire un film sur la Résistance."[29]

For the purpose of this chapter, which attempts a plausible aesthetic solution to the question of Malraux's renunciation of the novel, it is not important that after *Sierra de Teruel* Malraux the film director did not materialize. It is sufficient that at the end of his novelistic career two possible directions seem apparent: the *cinema* as a means of narrative expression, and the *essay* as a means of direct affirmation. Thus the movement that has been sketched in the body of this chapter would seem to be about to continue even after the last novel. Malraux sought for more than fifteen years a viable form of fiction, specifically a narrative technique which could give the events, the characters, and in particular his ideas on human transcendence a real immediacy for the reader. Having modified at several stages his novelistic style, he finally abandoned the genre, evidently convinced that such an ambition could never be achieved within a literary framework. Or so it was to appear until 1967 and the publication of the first segment of what was to become *Le Miroir des limbes*.[30]

CHAPTER EIGHT

On "Sierra de Teruel"

ce qui m'intéresse dans le cinéma
est le moyen de lier, artistiquement,
l'homme au monde (en tant que cosmos)
par un autre moyen que le langage.
(Malraux, letter to André Bazin, in
*Le Cinéma de l'Occupation et de la
Résistance*)[1]

In an interview with Michel Droit in 1967, at the time of the
publication of the *Antimémoires*, the first volume of *Le Miroir des
limbes*, Malraux insisted: "je suis très intéressé par la forme même des
Antimémoires. En définitive, je n'ai jamais écrit un roman pour écrire
un roman. J'ai poursuivi une sorte de méditation ininterrompue qui a
pris des formes successives, dont celle des romans."[2] He then went on
to emphasize that the work was supported by "une architecture
intérieure extrêmement forte."[3] Since the definitive publication of *Le
Miroir des limbes* in its entirety, the elements of that architecture – an
architecture the importance of which is recognized by the author
himself as decisively associated with his previous narrative evolution
– have been further illuminated and, as I suggested in a preceding
chapter, they would now seem to be the only valid point of departure
for any diachronic investigation of Malraux's fictional expression.

The narrative technique of the earliest of Malraux's writings had in
fact established his dual intention of creating an impression of
immediacy *and* of relating a precise imaginary experience to a wider
context. Thereafter, only the prophetic associative and stereoscopic
form of *Les Noyers de l'Altenburg* had in any way prepared readers for
the structure of *Le Miroir des limbes*. Indeed it is not until the 1943
novel that the primacy of his desire to translate appropriately his continuing preoccupation with the question "Qu'est-ce que l'homme?"
comes to pre-empt in large part the problem of immediacy and realism
in his fiction. Evidently, between the publication of *L'Espoir* in late
1937 and the beginning of the writing of *Les Noyers de l'Altenburg* in
1941, the nature of Malraux's narrative preoccupations had signi-

ficantly evolved. And yet, within that period, his only major aesthetic experiences were a film, *Sierra de Teruel*, and that film's theoretical sequel, *Esquisse d'une psychologie du cinéma*, one section (part 5) of which, however, it should be recalled, presents the only developed meditation on the nature of literary narrative which Malraux ever wrote. It is perhaps essentially against this background of narrative reflection that his cinematographic venture may well be most usefully re-examined.

It would be absurd to suggest that prior to 1937 Malraux was a *naïf* with regard to the cinema. However, its real force, as evoked by explicit reference in *La Tentation de l'Occident* and allusively in the novels – the explanation of its narrative superiority over literature – does in his view seem to lie entirely in its audiovisual ability to make a fictional world convincing.[4] And yet it may reasonably be proposed that the film that Malraux eventually made, after a miracle of effort in most adverse material circumstances amply recorded elsewhere,[5] is rather characterized by an *expansion* of the intrinsic realism of cinematographic language, an expansion essentially symptomatic of his desire to achieve an almost cosmic dimension in his work of art. This process of subordinating the camera, traditionally an unseen witness and recording instrument, to an experience of the imaginary and "un-real" possibilities of montage and image composition is lived at first hand by Malraux through the making of *Sierra de Teruel*. Thereafter he rationalizes the experience in the *Esquisse*, by which time serious cinema has become for him the manipulation of the mythical ("ruser avec le mythe").[6]

On an aesthetic level, it is therefore perhaps not unreasonable to contend that it was this encounter with a dichotomy, which in the cinema is more dramatically polarized than in literature, irrevocably conceptual, that led Malraux to focus his narrative attention more pronouncedly on the transcendent quality of the vision he wished to communicate, and which encouraged a decisive shift in emphasis in his work.

As Denis Marion, Franz-Josef Albersmeier, John Michalczyk, and Robert Thornberry have pointed out in their books, throughout the film there is certainly a high degree of realism, both in the visual and in the sound track. This is true to such an extent that an early showing led to some confusion among spectators about whether the film's authenticity was that of a real documentary, or at the very least the characters, non-professional actors. Moreover, it is true that a number of instances of Malraux's use of subjective camera angles and "affective" editing indicate his desire to project his spectator into an artistically created world. But at a deeper cinematographic level there seems to be a more significant, punctuated progression within the film, in which, by associating realistic elements stereoscopically, Malraux subverts realism in favour of a new dimension. Indeed, within the area of image composition, just such a procedure would seem to have been the most meaningful discovery Malraux made while making *Sierra de Teruel*. As he subsequently noted in the letter to Bazin cited above:

ce qui m'intéresse dans le cinéma est le moyen de lier, artistiquement, l'homme au monde (en tant que cosmos) par un autre moyen que le langage ... On peut toujours faire passer la caméra sur les nuages, et les Russes ont banalisé la chose; mais il y a des moyens plus subtils et plus aigus. Si je faisais un autre film, les images essentielles y seraient du type de la fourmi qui court sur le collimateur de la mitrailleuse.[7]

Although the image of the ant referred to has been frequently discussed, it remains a curious anomaly that critics have tended merely to relate this specifically *cinematographic* effect to the conclusion commonly drawn from the figurative network of insect imagery present in the novels. Marcel Martin writes that it emphasizes the general "innocence de la vie naturelle" within the devastating theatre of war; Pierre Galante interprets the image as being suggestive of man's fate.[8] But surely what is supremely important in this *audio*, as well as visual, context is quite simply that an ant is deaf! Malraux himself insisted on that very point when discussing aspects of the film-to-be with Louis Aragon, early in 1938:

Dans la zone du front, le bruit est si terrible que tous les êtres vivants, à part l'homme, s'enfuient. Seule la fourmi, qui est sourde, reste avec lui et se promène tranquillement jusque sur les mitrailleuses. Vous voyez cela en gros-plan ... la fourmi...?[9]

Rather than seeking to evoke a *parallel* between man and the insect, what the image – emphatically accompanied by the terrible rattle of war – is in fact designed to suggest obliquely, by the simple juxtaposition, but *contrast*, of two realistic elements, is man's uniqueness, that singularly lucid awareness with which he chooses to confront his fate.

Among several others, the close-up of the case of mounted butterflies hanging on the wall, which falls as a result of the reverberating bomb explosions, would seem to be of a similar type. What appears significant here is the fact that butterflies, characterized by a life cycle which includes provisional oblivion and resurrection, *fall* – any conventional associations are "dropped," so to speak. In terms of traditional immortality, there would seem to be a visually explicit subversion of the notion of transcendence and the substitution, through the all-powerful crash of the sound track, of a man- and death-oriented world, in which any evocation of transcendence must be limited to that precise scale.

Again, a not unrelated process may be noted in the intended montage of a sequence of the original scenario which was never filmed: the one in which cowbells are to be used as bombshells. The initial shots of the bomb-makers appropriating these bells would have dissociated the latter from their natural setting and established a new order in which the primacy of man's struggle was clear. Thereafter a transition was to be effected by a shot of a hand offering a cowbell in the foreground, with – in the background – a churchtower and its bell, massively outlined against the sky. The decisive gesture of the hand supplants in value the inert, petrified presence of the Church. This progression continues when the churchbell, ironically exalted by the angle-up shot counterpointing the sound of the picks engaged in its removal, is finally desacralized and resituated in the world of man, superbly revitalized as the ultimate bomb container!

Although it is just as valuable for us to consider the scenario as the film, since both are part of Malraux's narrative experience of this period, I do not intend in any way to support those who consider *Sierra de Teruel* to be "inachevé."[10] Indeed Malraux himself was at pains to point out, in the letter to Bazin, that "Les parties non tournées n'y sont pour rien ... je n'ai cessé de modifier scénario et dialogue, en fonction de la catastrophe qui approchait."[11] Rather, it is the integral structure of the film *tel quel* that I should now like to comment upon briefly.

First, at a superficial level, the structure of the film is dependent on a halting, "progression-by-sequence" movement, in which ellipsis – fundamental to the cinema in a guise already more aggressive than in literature – is still further exploited by Malraux. Claude-Edmonde Magny has described the device of ellipsis as the introduction into a narrative of "une discontinuité à la fois temporelle et spatiale propre à empêcher notre esprit d'organiser automatiquement le réel selon une certaine logique des apparences."[12] In this regard, the repeated disintegration of any continuous action in *Sierra de Teruel* in favour of an ultimate *a posteriori* intellectualization may be said to posit a level far beyond the immediate.

This possibility is further encouraged by a certain circularity in which the pervasiveness of *death* – in the first images that of Marcelino and in the concluding ones that of Saïdi – renders parenthetic all intervening human activity. Moreover, ceremonialized in the first instance by Peña's speech and in the later one by the accompanying cortege down the mountain, death is further abstracted by Malraux's refusal to portray the Fascist enemy except as a fugitive and shadowy destructive presence. In a visual experience such as film, visual absence is as powerful a sign as visual presence, and the conflict is no longer a purely political one.

However, beyond this limited circularity, the film's primary structure is an ascent, or rather a crescendo, in which sound and image come together pleonastically to confer an expansion.

In the course of the film, the initial war-derived sounds – of the siren and the stricken plane – gradually give way (though never entirely) to a realistically banal dialogue. The doubtful and provisional primacy of this vehicle of human communication, from which abstractions are conspicuously absent, is finally usurped by the elementary and wordless fraternal gesture of the closed fist salute. At the same time *music*, which during the previous scenes in the film had been confined entirely to the fictional level of the characters – Muñoz on the harmonica, snatches of flamenco and other songs – comes to dominate almost totally the final sequence of the descent of the mountainside, thus imposing a new level of perception.

According to Leavitt, music is basically ambivalent for Malraux: it may be either corrosive because of its serenity and intellectualism, or elevating if it is in a communal or revolutionary context.[13] In *Le Temps du mépris*, for example, Kassner encountered both effects: as he grew sensitive to the fraternity which underlay the physical separation imposed by the prison walls, music – previously painful to him because of "la fatalité des sons à imposer une désagrégation sans limites"[14] – finally became a salutary, spiritual experience:

Vautour et cachot s'enfonçaient sous une lourde cascade de chant funèbre jusqu'à une communion inépuisable, où la musique perpétuait tout passé en le délivrant du temps, en mêlant tout dans son évidence recueillie comme se fondent la vie et la mort dans l'immobilité du ciel étoilé.[15]

The parallel between this meditation of Kassner and the function of the eleven minutes of Darius Milhaud's "Cortège funèbre" with which *Sierra de Teruel* closes is, I think, important. The auditory realism of the body of the film's sound track has finally made way for a musical sublimation that, for the first time since the few semi-exergual bars accompanying the credit, is isolated from the narrative and directed openly at the sensibility of the listener. Emphasized in this way, music therefore indicates the terminal point in an itinerary which clearly extends beyond the merely material.

A comparable evolution can also be traced on the visual track. The small group which accompanies Marcelino's body as it leaves the snowfield becomes, by the end of the film, a massive procession down the mountainside. Moreover, the ingenuous authenticity of the initial pictures of the dead man finally gives way to all the accumulated symbolic power of a reconstituted artistico-Christian referential image.

With regard to the well-known concluding pictures of the reversed "Z" etched by the lines of villagers on the mountain path, other critics have already justifiably invoked Tintoretto's "Ascent to Calvary," and the ascending left to right, then right to left movement which Malraux specifically mentions in *Les Voix du silence*. But what should undoubtedly be the most crucial point elicited by such a comparison, beyond any pale imitation, beyond even the fact that the film repeats and then extends considerably in space the movement alluded to, seems to have gone unnoticed. It is that in Malraux's *kinetic* film medium, the movement, underlined repeatedly by a montage which uses Peña on horseback *ascending* as a constant visual contrast, is clearly a movement *downwards*. The transcendental dimension no longer culminates in the death and resurrection of Calvary, but is firmly rooted in man.

The film may be viewed then as a creation in which the inherent realism of the medium has allowed Malraux to focus more urgently his narrative technique on the expression of a metaphysical question. It would, therefore, be the preparation, execution, and subsequent theoretical conclusions of *Sierra de Teruel* which crystallized for him a need to translate more adequately the dimension of "le sacré" in his work, a dimension which was no longer simply an analogical backdrop for narratives rooted primarily in a quest for immediacy. In view of the substantial stylistic changes in his subsequent novel, *Les Noyers de l'Altenburg*, and with the considerable hindsight afforded by *Le Miroir des limbes*, *Sierra de Teruel* must now be considered as a singularly significant signpost in Malraux's narrative evolution.

CHAPTER NINE

On Feline Forms

Le chat s'en va, la queue
en point d'interrogation... (Malraux,
La Corde et les souris, 201)

"Est-il fée, est-il dieu?"[1] mused Baudelaire about that mysterious creature who/which is to be my central preoccupation through the pages which follow, insisting, as have so many others, on the multifaceted *insaisissable* quality which seems above all to typify the representatives of that particular species. And it is textual investigation across Malraux's writings of this same chameleon-like ability of the cat to take on very different avatars which brings one to posit an important and fundamental evolution in that writer's vision of the world.

There is no doubt that in terms of longevity the cat or felid, with a fossil history that stretches back some forty million years, evolved as one of the earliest of modern mammals. Parenthetically, but with delightful coherence for certain associations in Malraux, the largest of these prehistoric examples is called a *Smilodon*! The cat's place in legend is apparent from at least Egyptian times onwards, as Pasht and Ra, then Diana and Freya, the Teutonic Venus, were all associated with feline attributes. Thereafter, an intuited occult resonance saw the beast as a frequent sacrifice at religious festivals or else as a regular candidate for dissection and subsequent "medicinal" use. Certainly, the Oriental explanation of the origin of the cat leaves us in doubt as to its disquieting and anti-conventional heritage. In a story which appears to relate to the Ark, despite the fact that the Cat is conspicuously absent from any page of the Bible, it is told that at the beginning of the voyage the animals rested peacefully in their private staterooms. The first, eventually, to issue forth was the monkey who, disregarding the clearly enunciated rule of racial purity, by various machinations persuaded the lioness to forget her vows of fidelity. The result of this transgression of natural laws was the birth of the Cat! and historical man, especially literary man, has never been the same since.

There was Mohammed's white Muezza, there was the topaz-eyed cat that vied with Laura for Petrarch's favours, Dick Whittington's pet, Montaigne's old grey, suitably supercilious, companion, Dr Johnson's Hodge, and Hinse of Hinsefield, the wise ally of Sir Walter Scott, red stately Micetto – Chateaubriand's gift from the Pope himself – Hugo's languorous Chanoine, the veritable dynasties of felids which ruled Gautier's home and Baudelaire's heart, as well as Loti's awesome twosome, Moumotte Blanche and Moumotte Chinoise.

And yet, despite the above brief inventory of the Cat's recurrent, reverberating presence in history, legend, religion, and literature, it is my contention that *no major artist* has ever been as decisively cat-coded as André Malraux.

From the very first texts, through the novels and the art works, right up to the monumental *Miroir des limbes*, the insistent, anonymous, feline presence – particularly at key moments – is remarkable; in addition, for more than half a century, Malraux characteristically signed himself to his intimates with the sketched outline of a cat. Further, more marginal, allusions to pointed ears, soft fur, and enigmatic tails are enriched by repeated specific reference to figures such as Perrault's "Chat botté," Picasso's "Chat doré," and Lewis Carroll's Cheshire variety. Previous Malraux commentators have, admittedly, pointed out, perhaps too tentatively, a certain affection for the species; some have already meaningfully associated it with the author's invocation of the term "farfelu." However, it may well be that all have remained insensitive to a series of notable re-evaluations which decisively mark different points in Malraux's itinerary. In a bizarre, yet totally innocent, perversion of Alice's flamingo croquet mallets, I shall, in the following pages, brandish Malraux's cat as a barometer to significant changes in atmosphere in that author's writings, and perhaps, ultimately, if the cat barometer will stand the pressure of the enquiry, develop any findings towards more universal conclusions.

Symptomatically, a black cat appears, if only as a passing frame of reference, on the first page of Malraux's first published literary text, "Mobilités," even before *Lunes en papier*: "Sectionnant la végétation ouatée semblable à une fourrure de chat noir, brillent les raies de deux routes fixées, à leur carrefour, par un énorme champignon d'acier."[2]

Subsequently, the cat, ever characterized by prevailing gratuitousness at this time, becomes in *Lunes en papier* the outward form of the protagonist, the delicious "génie du lac, pelote à épingles en forme de chat"[3] whose tail in sleep habitually traces cartoons in the sand. For the most part, the tail chooses to caricaturize the cat's principal enemies, the dreaded "aérostats" or balloons. The moment of truth eventually arrives when the balloons, charmed by the plausible patter of the feline hero, are inveigled into imbibing hugely excessive, if enviable, quantities of "très vieille fine Champagne," and fall into a stupor: "Alors, à petits pas, le chat revint. Il riait. Il prit les ballons par le tube comme des grains de raisin par la queue, et, s'essayant à cueillir un supplice digne de punir leur férocité, choisit la pendaison."[4]

However, the creature was really seeking to indulge his longtime "basse passion," which was a craving to see the balloons put out their tongues. Alas! to no avail, for despite the cord around their necks "Elles s'obstinaient! Donc la vie du chat était irrémédiablement manquée."[5] With gentle irony the cat's own weight, as in frustration he hangs himself, causes the balloons' tongues finally to appear, and his failure is further emphasized as his own emerges involuntarily!

Further textual investigation would merely substantiate the contention that in the early writings the cat is an important *comic* element in a fantastic world where death is undoubtedly present, but is stylized to a degree that robs it of its sting. Indeed, one could extend this to suggest that through its pointed ears – a common feature of nearly all of Malraux's later *human* characters who are blessed with some "farfelu" tendency, however minimal – its soft fur and its strange power, the cat in these early texts is part of a wide-ranging diabolical fauna that is in no way terrifying, but is rather made up, for the most part, of quaint, playful little creatures.[6]

Before Indochina, as Clara confirms and as we have seen in an earlier chapter, the youthful Malraux had not yet really been touched by suffering, let alone death.[7] After Indochina, particularly at Banteai-Chmar, "la Forteresse du Chat"[8] as he conveniently relates, after this confrontation with the hostility within raw nature *and* between men, both potentially lethal, there is first a decisive hardening and refining of his often cat-associated humour, evidenced primarily in his aggressively satirical journalism of that period, before a clear diminishing. A not dissimilar evolution has already been traced with regard to other manifestations of the comic.

Of course, Malraux's personal tendency towards the whimsical remained with him to some degree throughout his life; one has only to recall the innumerable caricatures drawn during lengthy meetings of

Ministers in the sixties. And although in the immediate aftermath of the Indochina experience there was a shift in accent, there certainly remain conspicuous examples of his playful humour. One, in particular, is worth recalling here since it takes the form of a dialogue between a bibliophile and, inevitably, a cat – I refer to that introduction to a rare-book catalogue,[9] written in 1929, and cited earlier in this volume.

Increasingly, however, such gratuitous comic mythomania was rigorously exorcized by the author from his serious novelistic writing. Certain titillating Clappique episodes disappear as manuscript becomes published work, and the similarly playful Rensky is completely edited out of *Les Conquérants* for the 1949 version. Just as we discovered in a previous chapter with regard to "butterflies," the amusement of the aesthete pales before the painful rictus of mortal man.

Let us now examine how the frame of reference to be associated with cats is altered in a period approximately from Indochina to the early post-World War II years, when the accompanying notion of the "farfelu" is inseparable from a confrontation with man's tragic condition.

Undoubtedly the character who is most often associated with a feline presence is inevitably the character who is the prime embodiment of the "farfelu" of this period – Clappique. Cats insist on crossing his erratic path, he instinctively projects feline traits onto the women he frequents, and it is his cat-coded stories which are the regular enchantment of both Ferral and Valérie. The significance of this feline presence is only illuminated clearly when Clappique emerges from the unpleasant confrontation with reality during the Shan-Tung arms-buying episode: "le visage du baron était à peine visible, mais le grand chat lumineux, enseigne du *Black Cat*, l'entourait comme une auréole."[10]

This image of the Baron, symbolically effaced in any real terms by a feline fantasy in neon, is far more potentially destructive in terms of man's situation in the world than anything encountered in *Lunes en papier* or *Royaume-farfelu*. Indeed, its importance is such that it recurs revealingly in *L'Espoir*, as the garish, artificial, brilliance of the sign of the El Gato tavern represents in Shade's mind the ultimate futility of even pseudo-heroic actions in the war which he is reporting.[11]

Less emphasized, perhaps, but nevertheless scattered throughout the novels, are fleeting indications of the degree to which the largely comical creatures of yesteryear have been replaced by the bitter indifference of a cat who seems to evoke an ongoing natural process in direct contrast to the patent mortality of man. We read, for example, in *L'Espoir* of the execution of three Fascists: "Les trois hommes avaient été fusillés dans une rue voisine; les corps étaient tombés sur le ventre, têtes au soleil, pieds à l'ombre. Un tout petit chat mousseux penchait ses moustaches sur la flaque de sang de l'homme au nez plat."[12]

However, perhaps it is in fact Ferral, in *La Condition humaine*, who implicitly reveals the extent to which the laughing cat of the early years has now been reduced to a mockingly fugitive feline leer. Valérie, Ferral's preferred partner, knows *Alice in Wonderland* by heart, and it is with regard to that work's Cheshire cat that Ferral sees a link substantiated – or rather, perhaps, *un*substantiated – in Valérie: "votre sourire me fait penser au fantôme du chat qui ne se matérialisait jamais, et dont on ne voyait qu'un ravissant sourire de chat flottant dans l'air."[13] As elsewhere in his life, in his erotic manoeuvres with Valérie, Ferral is seeking a self-fulfilment that is unattainable; Valérie remains impermeably and inevitably the Other. There is ultimately no contact, no mastery. Valérie's smile, however charming, is in truth the unanswerable condemnation of man's fate. The cat, it seems, has become the very symbol of the Absurd.

Thereafter, it is not until 1967, with the commencement of the fragmented publication of that work eventually to be entitled *Le Miroir des limbes*, that there is projected, most powerfully, a new role for Malraux's cats. Certainly, from the very first page onwards, there are cats everywhere; moreover, they even proliferate and reproduce from edition to edition. There are the regiments of cats at Agincourt, the Abyssinian cat given to Pope Gregory, the one at Vauvenargues which recalls, in its turn, the Lion-Goddess of Luxor, Queen Sebeth's giant beast, the black cat at the United Nations, sorcerers' cats, cats which salute and speak, green cats.

In many cases Malraux makes it patently clear that the cat, once associated, first humoristically, then tragically, with death, now divorces itself, flees, from any substantial contact with that experience, situates itself voluntarily elsewhere. Grigri, the General's cat, "s'est enfui comme s'il avait peur" when suicide was mentioned, Méry's cat "s'agite" whenever his ailing master talks of death.[14] In the course of Malraux's visit to the medium, Madame Khodari Pacha, the latter during her meditation has cause to speak in similar terms: "Le chat miaule, tourne sur lui-même, saute sur mes genoux. Je le caresse. – Ne vous inquiétez pas, dit-elle: il se comporte toujours de cette façon quand je vois la mort."[15]

A first indication of the new value to be attached to a feline presence is provided in one of the several cat stories which punctuate a dinner at Colombey, given for Malraux and Geoffrey de Courcel. Malraux relates:

L'histoire du chat que je préférais, dis-je – je ne sais plus si elle est de Louise de Vilmorin, de Jean Cocteau ou de moi – est celle-ci:
   Au coin du feu un vieil Anglais, sa femme et leur chat noir. Le chat regarde l'homme et lui dit: "Ta femme t'a trompé." L'Anglais décroche son fusil de chasse et tue la femme. Le chat s'en va, la queue en point d'interrogation et dit "J'ai menti."
–L'histoire doit être de vous, dit le général.[16]

   Beyond the conventional overtones of feline arrogance, independence, and immorality, the essential element here may well be the visual sign of the question mark informed by the cat's tail. Clearly it is this quizzical quality which would explain Malraux's renewed predilection for the Cheshire cat. Already invoked with regard to the Absurd, Lewis Carroll's cat is now more properly recognized by Malraux as the very incarnation of the enigmatic. Certainly this is the quality which Alice stresses, for the cat is not only enigmatic in appearance (it had "very long claws and a great many teeth" but its constant grin made it look "good-natured"),[17] it is also enigmatic in its responses:

"Would you tell me please, which way I ought to walk from here?" asked Alice.
   "That depends a good deal on where you want to get to," said the Cat.
   "I don't much care where," said Alice.
   "Then it doesn't much matter which way you walk," said the Cat.
   "So long as I get somewhere," Alice added as an explanation.
   "Oh you're sure to do that," said the Cat, "if you only walk long enough."[18]

The Cat is also enigmatic in its actions ("I growl when I'm pleased and wag my tail when I'm angry"), in its departure (it leaves "a grin without a cat"), and with regard to death ("How do you behead a cat without a body?" ponders the King of Hearts' executioner).[19]
   The Cheshire Cat then seems, if not necessarily impervious to death, at least to present to the world the image of a cheerfully lucid question mark. It is precisely these qualities, of the lucid and the interrogative in harmonious balance, which characterize Malraux's rediscovery of the Cheshire Cat, just as he slips into a coma in the concluding paragraph of Le Miroir des limbes:

Peu avant de perdre conscience, j'ai vu mon chat Fourrure, et entrevu dans l'obscurité le sourire du chat invisible d' *Alice au pays des merveilles*. A l'instant de basculer ... j'ai senti la mort s'éloigner; pénétré, envahi, possédé, comme par une ironie inexplicablement réconciliée, qui fixait au passage la face usée de la mort.[20]

Those same curious beasts which once joyfully traced caricatures in the sand have now cast off their subsequent association with the bitter irony of the Absurd. There is no clear affirmative substitute, merely a rejection of the negative, and the acceptance of question or limbo as the proper condition of man. This then is the terminal point in Malraux's cat-accompanied journey – fugitively and figuratively glimpsed at the end of *Le Miroir des limbes*, it will be directly enunciated in the final non-fiction work, *L'Homme précaire et la littérature*.

Malraux's feline forms bring us, at the last, however tentatively, to their author's ultimate vision of the world. For him Man is coming, must come, to live without pain, within the perplexing dimension of a seemingly oblivion-oriented condition, an unending dialectic which subsumes, *perhaps* transcends, rather than confronts, Anguish and Mirth, Life and Death:

L'aléatoire n'exige pas l'absurde, mais un agnosticisme de l'esprit: le tragique n'est pas sa dernière instance, et sans doute n'en a-t-il pas d'autre que lui-même. Pour lui l'homme n'est qu'objet d'interrogation.[21]

CHAPTER TEN

On Death and Dying

nous ne pouvons ignorer que toute vie
est promise à la mort. Cela me semble
un objet de réflexion tout à fait
différent de celui du trépas. (Malraux,
in conversation with Georges Suffert
and Jean Montalbetti)[1]

In an invertebrate Godless world, such as that envisioned by many
writers of this century, death has become both terribly final and
dreadfully present. However, few authors have focused quite so
unrelentingly on the subject as André Malraux in his unflinching
novelistic quest for some new and positive value with which to
confront the anguish of the Absurd.

Indeed, even beyond his writings and reflections, Malraux's own
life seems to project increasingly a tragic ongoing encounter with the
patent mortality of those he knew and often loved. The violent death
of his grandfather, his father's suicide, the fatal accident to Josette
Clotis, the disappearance of his brother, the crash which cost his two
sons their lives, to say nothing of the loss of a string of friends, and
the persecution, war, executions, reprisals which characterized
Indochina, Spain, the Dordogne, and Alsace – all were circumstances
which contrived to inform richly his imagination with the very
vulnerable flesh of reality. And yet the fullness of this enrichment, the
nuances which Malraux recognizes and develops, has often been
brushed aside by readings which simply see *death* in Malraux as a
single uncomplicated reference point, a mere monolithic signpost to
the Absurd.

Few, happily, choose to ignore the nuances quite as blatantly as
Roger Garaudy in his unbalanced, politically slanted, study which
stretches credulousness beyond a maximum, as he presents death in
Malraux as simply some crude symbol of "reactionary defeatism" and
"an ethic of decadence." Extraordinarily, for Garaudy in 1948, the
sole interest of Malraux's vision of the world lay in its moribund

creator, who had become "a medium for a dying class and a dying social system because he furnishes a psychological transposition and a metaphysical justification of their disorder and agony."[2]

There is without doubt rather more subtlety in Serge Gaulupeau's essay *André Malraux et la mort*. Nevertheless, for Gaulupeau, death in Malraux's work is still limited in its ramifications, and is essentially to be seen only in terms of an ambiguous metaphysical experience: "La Mort est ambiguë parce qu'elle est maîtresse d'absurdité et de sens en même temps."[3] Although most critics would subscribe to such a duality, the study might well have been more comprehensive had Gaulupeau chosen to differentiate more radically, as does Malraux himself, between metaphysical Death and human dying.

Despite being similarly preoccupied above all with Death with a capital "D," perhaps the most sensitive analysis to date is that of Thomas Jefferson Kline.[4] Kline monitors with careful scholarship an evolution in Malraux's attitude towards Death through an examination of associated image patterns, pointing to a progression from an anguished impasse to the ultimate attainment of Grace. Perhaps, however, although the essential direction of this itinerary is undoubtedly plausible, it may have been wiser to stop short of such a positive interpretation of its terminal point, and posit only that what is finally proffered by Malraux is better characterized as, at the very most, aleatory or interrogative.

To my knowledge only G.T. Harris in his too brief (alas!) "Note on *Le Miroir des limbes*: A Convoy of Utopias and Aspirations"[5] presents with any force the fact of dying in Malraux as potentially very different to Death. And yet there is an important distinction here on which Malraux himself insisted with pointed frequency. For example, in *Le Miroir des limbes* he returns to it on no less than three occasions. First, while discussing his imprisonment by the Germans during World War II, he declares: "le trépas me semblait banal. Ce qui m'intéressait, c'était la mort"; and later, in response to a question from de Gaulle about the nature of death, Malraux proposes that it is best figured as "la déesse du sommeil," but adds that dying itself, however, is for him of no account: "Le trépas ne m'a jamais intéressé."[6] Towards the end of that volume he reiterates the same point of view when he insists on the misguided character of some of the analyses of which his readers have been guilty: "L'importance que j'ai donnée au caractère métaphysique de la mort m'a fait croire obsédé par le trépas."[7] Moreover, he returns to what is clearly a qualititative differentiation of some considerable significance on other occasions during interviews; in particular, in addition to the exergual example preceding the present chapter, during a conversation with Michel Droit published in *Le Figaro littéraire*. There he admits readily that death does fascinate him, but stresses once again: "pas la mort en tant que trépas, car sous cet angle la mort m'est indifférente. Le fait que la mort existe."[8]

Since Malraux does choose very deliberately to separate, and even oppose, *dying* ("le trépas") and *Death* ("la Mort"), it would seem worthwhile to explore just how much import that emphatic distinction does indeed have for an interpretation of his writings. With such a dichotomy in mind it may even be possible to go further and suggest that detailed investigation of the several "death experiences" described by Malraux offers a provocative invitation to reconsider basic assumptions of traditional Malraux exegesis.

From the beginning, the *écrits farfelus* provide early pointers to the differing characteristics of dying and Death, those two facets of mortality which are to preoccupy us in this chapter. In 1920, in Malraux's first published literary text, "Mobilités," dying is presented, however playfully, as a brief, uncomplicated, banal instant, where any "illuminating" quality is dissociated and subsequent:

Une boule aérienne passe, endormie, les pattes repliées, et se crève à l'une des pointes du croissant.

   Alors pour l'éclairer? – une petite flamme très blanche sort de chacune de ses extrémités et s'y suspend...[9]

On another occasion, in *Lunes en papier*, the act of dying, somewhat differently, is coloured with pathos and irony. The Cat, who is the mysterious "génie du lac," aches to satisfy its particular craving ("sa basse passion"), which is to see some balloons poke out their tongues. It therefore "hangs" the balloons but, as we have seen, is ridiculously unsuccessful because their obdurate tongues refuse to emerge. A further ironic twist follows as the disillusioned Cat hangs itself in despair, and its own tongue comes out!

On the other hand, Death is portrayed in the same book as a totally insensitive ("complètement insensible"), but tyrannical and powerful, emperor, one that is also already disturbingly enigmatic. For the seven Deadly Sins, having conspired to kill Death, become depressed once the deed is done and lament, asking themselves repeatedly: "Pourquoi avons-nous tué la Mort?"[10] The tacit implication would seem to be that Death, in addition to its destructive aspect, also invests life with some quality, possibly an intensity, that is vital. This ambivalence and aggrandizement of Death contrast already with the banality and lack of serious substance that have been initially related to dying, announcing a polarization that will be maintained in the novels which follow.

In *Les Conquérants*, the first of these, Garine seems for the most part curiously disinterested in his encroaching illness. Even when he does demonstrate some preoccupation with death, it is solely in meta-physical terms: "L'absurde retrouve ses droits…"[11] Although his fate is apparently inevitable, the actual moment of death is not described. Nevertheless, the symbolic final embrace of the narrator and the dying protagonist is once again symptomatic of the ultimate ordinari-ness of the event: "Je cherche dans ses yeux la joie que j'ai cru voir; mais il n'y a rien de semblable, rien qu'une dure et pourtant fraternelle gravité."[12] It is a leave-taking which is affectionate and solemn, but devoid of that intensity that the narrator had both expected and sought.

There is a similar lack of intensity confirmed in *La Voie royale* by Perken with regard to his own imminent death: "Il y a des moments où j'ai l'impression que cette histoire n'a aucun intérêt."[13] In fact the only real "drama" seems to be in the pain of the injury, a pain which is even exalted, but rather because it demonstrates continuing life than because it prefigures the end. Thus Perken feels "une joie profonde à chacun des battements de son sang," and Claude recognizes more explicitly that "la souffrance protégeait son ami contre la mort: tant qu'il souffrait, il vivait."[14]

And yet for Malraux, in sharp and noteworthy contrast, it is precisely with a sense of intensity that Death is to be associated; indeed it is this alone which fundamentally separates Western civilization from its counterpart in the East, as Malraux concedes when quoting Nehru in *Le Miroir des limbes*: "l'intensité de la civilisation occidentale vient de la mort. Dans l'aventure cosmique qu'est ici [l'Asie] l'univers, la mort ne donne aucune intensité à la vie."[15]

The apparent gulf between dying and Death that Malraux seeks to establish from very early in his career would seem to be further attested by comparison of the original manuscript of *La Voie royale* with the published version. In the former only there occurs among the final few lines a sentence which reads: "La galerie souterraine était là, et aucun être humain ne pouvait s'interposer entre elle et lui."[16] The elimination of such an image as this subterranean gallery appears to indicate an unwillingness to project the experience of dying as some rite of passage between Life and Death. By rejecting any continuous progression of this sort, Malraux separates the two poles more totally, preferring to place the experience of dying within the experience of living, thus isolating Death as qualitatively different. As I shall stress later, this revealing omission from the published version of *La Voie royale* finds a more positive amplification in *L'Espoir*, when, on two occasions, the reader is confronted with a declaration that maintains that there is an interval of an hour or so after dying before the soul appears. Death and dying are thus not only not linked, they are not of the same species; they are, therefore, consequently and meaningfully dissociated in time.

Nowhere in Malraux's writings are a character's final hours so closely monitored as in *La Condition humaine*, and on three separate occasions. In each instance a character seems to be seeking, at least momentarily, through a certain quality of death, a personal apotheosis; in each instance the Absolute that is desired is shown to be a myth, a twentieth-century grail that may be glimpsed but not seized. More specifically with regard to our present thesis, the choosing or embracing of a particular death is presented as potentially self-deceiving, since one's dying moments in Malraux have no more *ultimate* value than brushing one's teeth; it is only a further, certainly significant, aspect of one's life, but does not constitute *the* arena in which to respond satisfactorily to the Absurd.

Tchen is obsessed with the world of death from the beginning of the novel; indeed, it seems to make up his entire waking experience: "il était seul avec la mort."[17] He sees in the coincidence of a death given and a death received the possibility of a supreme *Instant*, and therefore arranges to throw himself under Chang-Kai-Chek's car with a bomb clutched to his breast. It is this yearning for a final, total, consummation of his life that generates the almost erotic ecstasy which accompanies the act: "Tchen serra la bombe sous son bras avec reconnaissance," "Il courut vers elle [la voiture] avec une joie d'extatique, se jeta dessus, les yeux fermés."[18]

The terrible absurdity, the ghastly failure, is that, first, Chang is not in the car and, second, Tchen does not kill himself, although he is dreadfully mutilated – "de la chair hachée."[19] However, worse is to follow. Having managed to raise his gun to his mouth in order to finish himself off, Tchen finds he can no longer act, no longer has the strength. His dying moment, that supreme experience he had cherished and prepared, becomes abjectly passive, a purely reflex action as the result of a policeman's brutal kick: "Un furieux coup de talon d'un autre policier crispa tous ses muscles: il tira sans s'en apercevoir."[20] It is surely not without significance that the character who invested in the style of his dying the most value is presented by Malraux as the most pathetically unsuccessful, with regard both to the death he sought to administer and to that which he sought to receive. Malraux's contention appears to be that a life in which the mode of one's dying is paramount is liable to prove a sadly futile waste.

After a life devoted to the revolutionary cause Kyo too, at the very end, sees in dying not merely the closing scene of life, but something elevated: "mourir pouvait être un acte exalté, la suprême expression d'une vie à quoi cette mort ressemblait tant."[21] And, once again, there is clear indication that the character may be attributing too much significance to simple physical circumstance. For Malraux chooses very deliberately to negate the final gesture of fraternity with which Kyo sought to conclude and consecrate a life lived for his fellow men: "au moment où il voulait se raccrocher à lui [Katow], suffoquant, il sentit toutes ses forces le dépasser."[22] Just as, elsewhere, a character's dying experience is presented in terms other than absolute, other than perfect, other than those desired by the character in question; once again the attentive reader is confronted, however briefly, by a demystification of the notion that an individual's death is in any way decisively significant. Thus, not only is the ceremonial, saintly, position ("Allongé sur le dos, les bras ramenés sur la poitrine...") Kyo had adopted a short time previously disrupted, but also an earlier reiteration of the standard myths ("Il est facile de mourir quand on ne meurt pas seul." – "Mort saturée de ce chevrotement fraternel...") finds itself devalued at the last.[23] But let us be clear. It is not in any way Kyo's life that is invalidated here, only the fallacy that dying is some sort of crucial mystery.

Katow is often regarded as the character with whom Malraux explores most sympathetically the question of a *heroic* attitude towards dying. Imprisoned without hope in the school courtyard, facing torture and a painful death, Katow has the consolation of an easy escape available through his cyanide pill. However, the charity which has constantly characterized his life to date is seen appropriately, and with strict logic, to colour his final hours too, as he gives up his relatively easy death – twice – to the two terrified Chinese. But, as well as fixing even more forcefully Katow's generosity – in a Cornelian sense, of course – this act offers as its evident corollary that, for the authentic "hero," the actual mode of dying is accepted as variable and comparatively unimportant in terms of its eventual form. What is important is one's attitude towards life in all its facets, under the ineluctable assault of Death. This is further underlined thereafter, as Katow is thwarted in his subsequent intention to attack the guards who come to take him away and has, finally, to accept the certainty of being burned alive in the locomotive furnace: "Allons! supposons que je sois mort dans un incendie."[24] The privileged moments, *in life*, of sacrifice and selflessness are now past; only the banality of the curtain's descent remains.

With far more emphasis than in the earlier writings, each death in *La Condition humaine* admits the inadequacy of that experience to provide any answer to the final absurdity that is Death; but none, with the sole exception of Tchen, in any way discounts the considerable merit of the life assumed.

This would also be true, of course, with regard to Hernandez in *L'Espoir*, whose moral and spiritual heroism is not at all jeopardized by a certain loss of lucidity as he awaits his turn for the firing squad. Certainly he has himself already registered the ironic inevitability and total commonness of dying: "Tous mourront. Il a vu une de ses amies mourir d'un cancer généralisé; son corps était châtain, comme ses cheveux; et elle était médecin."[25]

From such a vantage point Hernandez contemplates the Fascist executioners, who become ridiculous facsimiles of "les ordonnateurs des pompes funèbres"; even the condemned prisoners who precede him in the fatal line are observed with bitter humour: "Sauf au cirque, Hernandez n'a jamais vu un homme sauter en arrière."[26] But still more revealing is that moment, already examined in another context, when Hernandez's consciousness wavers and, thereafter, the reader discovers that the strange events being narrated are in fact only the direct transposition of figments of the imagination of Hernandez and his companions rendered erratic by nervousness:

Trois fascistes viennent prendre trois prisonniers. Ils les mènent devant la fosse, reculent ...

Ils font un saut périlleux en arrière. Le peloton tire, mais ils sont déjà dans la fosse. Comment peuvent-ils espérer s'en échapper? Les prisonniers rient nerveusement.

Ils n'auront pas à s'en échapper. Les prisonniers ont vu le saut d'abord, mais le peloton a tiré avant. Les nerfs.[27]

The transparent and collective human-ness of this illusion confirms that the event is not tinged with any possibility whatsoever of some "semi-transcendental" illumination. On the contrary, dying is essentially a basic physical experience. If, as here, coloured with heightened awareness on account of the ubiquitous looming shadow of Death, then it is at the very most another example of those various *situations extrêmes* that Malraux investigated throughout his work. It is, therefore, as suggested earlier, more accurately associated with life, in a world, however, where life is what it is because it has been impregnated by Death.

This resituating of dying in a different arena to Death was a conclusion we adumbrated from our first reference to Malraux's *écrits farfelus*. It is perhaps at its most obvious in Malraux's re-creations of the Spanish Civil War. There, in *L'Espoir*, the act of dying is again subordinated to the awful truth that Death projects indiscriminately; only after an intervening period of time does the superficial human mask give way and the soul appear:

Comme Marcelino avait été tué d'une balle dans la nuque il n'était pas ensanglanté. Malgré la tragique fixité des yeux que personne n'avait fermés, malgré la lumière sinistre, le masque était beau.

Il faut au moins une heure pour qu'on commence à voir l'âme, dit-elle [une serveuse] ... Magnin pensait à la phrase qu'il venait d'entendre, qu'il avait entendue sous tant de formes en Espagne; c'est seulement une heure après leur mort, que, du masque des hommes, commence à sourdre leur vrai visage.[28]

That this separation in time was in some way fundamental to Malraux's concept of the ramifications of mortality is suggested by its retention in the opening sequence of *Sierra de Teruel*, the film that he made of the same Spanish combat. This time it is one of the village women clustered around Marcelino's body who recalls: "C'est seulement une heure après la mort qu'on commence à voir l'âme."[29]

Not surprisingly, an identical dichotomy to that traced above exists in Malraux's final novel, *Les Noyers de l'Altenburg*. In particular there is further articulation of the intensity which awareness of Death, of metaphysical *néant*, brings to our encounters. The passages narrating the escape from the tank ditch and, above all, the inhuman gas attack are meaningful because they reveal to the protagonists the desperate value of life.

Yet again, however, as in each of the novels, a character's actual experience of dying robs that precise moment of any unnatural accentuation. Of course Dietrich Berger's chosen death demonstrates his will and resolve by his provision of both strychnine and revolver – just in case. But, equally, his death is portrayed as above all a continuation of his chosen life: "la résolution par quoi il avait choisi la mort, une mort qui ressemblait à sa vie."[30] And, even more coherently for my present argument, it is a death experience which is more or less explicitly subsumed into the nature of things. Elsewhere it is a cat or a butterfly,[31] on this occasion an ant which, running disinterestedly over the agents of death, furnishes its own silent commentary: "mon grand-père avait fumé soit avant de prendre le véronal, soit avant de s'endormir. Sur le bord du cendrier, une fourmi courait. Elle avait continué en ligne droite son chemin, grimpé sur le revolver déposé là."[32]

This fractured state of mortality which I have sketched through Malraux's writings, in which dying and Death are given very different emphasis, reaches its most clearly enunciated state in the autobiographical section of *Le Miroir des limbes* originally entitled *Lazare*.

Already in Garine, Perken, and even Kassner in *Le Temps du mépris*, the reader has received glimpses of the precise physical degeneration that heralds imminent death. *Lazare*, from the beginning, sets out to record with considerable technical awareness the phenomenology of dying. The dreadful annihilation recounted in the Bolgako attack is recalled from *Les Noyers de l'Altenburg* with clinical lack of comment. The particular deaths of various historical figures and friends – Méry, de Gaulle, Christ, Socrates, Josette Clotis, Groethuysen – are logged by Malraux in much the same way as he then sets down his own immediate deterioration: "En attendant, sclérose des nerfs périphériques et menace sur le cervelet, donc menace de paralysie."[33] What we are being given is a scientific scrutiny devoid of any of the novelistic craving for meaning and merit. Malraux thus divorces himself even more clearly from his characters, whose deaths are in each case tinged with frustration or disillusionment, and espouses an attitude towards "le trépas" that is ultimately dismissive. Only Death is able to radiate a resonance that reverberates significantly for the human condition.

It therefore comes as no surprise that, at the end of Malraux's chronicle, the recording of the banal certainty of each individual's death fades into oblivion, and is replaced by the far more momentous enigma of metaphysical Death. The primacy of the latter is in no doubt as references to dying retreat ("la face usée de la mort")[34] and the narrative closes on Malraux's final image prior to losing consciousness, the symbol of the Cheshire Cat's quizzical smile: "j'ai … entrevu dans l'obscurité le sourire du chat invisible d'*Alice au pays des merveilles*."[35] Ethereal, intangible, interrogative, it is the emanation of Death that reigns supreme, and not the fact of dying.

It is, for Malraux, because of Death, not dying, that life is a *question* – in both French senses of the word; but it is also because of Death, not dying, that life can be a personal triumph. Recognition, therefore, of Malraux's dismissive extradition of "dying" brings with it necessarily, not only a more precise limitation of the Absurd, but above all a refreshed awareness of that author's commitment to the glorious passion of human life. "J'ai appris aussi qu'une vie ne vaut rien, mais que rien ne vaut une vie."[36]

CHAPTER ELEVEN

On Oratory

Il n'est pas possible ... que de gens
qui ont besoin de parler et de gens qui
ont besoin d'entendre, ne naisse pas
un style... (Malraux, *L'Espoir*, 51)

Rhetoric and oratory, the art of using words effectively and the practice of that art in public speech, are associated notions that have undergone a strange change in destiny since the halcyon days of Antiquity. In ancient Greece and Rome "chairs" in these disciplines were necessarily endowed in all large cities and their most eminent holders were celebrated unreservedly. Indeed, despite the gradual move away from elevated expression towards more common speech noted by historians of the subject, rhetoric remained a fundamental principle of education in most of Western Europe until well into the nineteenth century. It may even be that it was only with the advent of the audiovisual media, particularly television, with their accompanying modifications in style of delivery, that "oratory" and "rhetoric" finally took on the pejorative resonance that seems for the most part to characterize them today. Nevertheless, even within comparatively recent times, the continuing possibility of public oral persuasion has been evidenced to devastating effect in two World Wars, proof that, even if despised as a concept, great oratory can survive in our time.

Be that as it may, it does seem curiously anomalous that during this same period of relative demise at least one persuasive rhetorical mode, the serious novel, was continuing to prosper and allowing its exponents to communicate their attitudes more effectively and more widely than in any other form. It was obviously recognition of just such a fact that encouraged authors, Camus and Sartre for example, to give fictional substance to their thought in works of literature. Novelistic "rhetoric," it would seem, was not suffering from quite the same malaise as oral.

However, there does exist a rare instance of a creative talent for whom such nuances scarcely seemed to exist, one who encompassed in his *oeuvre* the full potentiality of the rhetorical traditions of yesteryear. For André Malraux – novelist, essayist, *and* orator – the lines which now seek to distinguish between written and oral remain for the most part just as blurred as in Antiquity. In his novels the concrete, historically contextualized, actions only take on full significance in the light of the accompanying reflective dialogue; in the best of his speeches there is often a rigorous formal structure that invites comparison with certain of his novels.

Malraux the novelist has long been consecrated by the critics. And yet, although it is not particularly original to remark on the quality of Malraux's oratory,[1] there does not exist, to my knowlege, any extended study of this manifestation of his rhetoric. Strangely so, since it soon becomes apparent that an analysis of Malraux as public speaker has compelling overtones for his literature, even beyond an enormous intrinsic interest. For Malraux, in his speeches, will be seen to be touched by that same quality of genius that had already marked him out in other areas as one of the most remarkable figures of this century.

Certainly the range of Malraux's contributions as a speaker is remarkable: over some fifty years he addressed audiences all over the world on matters cultural, political, social, moral, philosophical, and even legal. Already during his trial in Saigon, as even the generally unsympathetic commentator from *L'Impartial* was compelled to admit, Malraux was able to demonstrate a precocious gift for oral presentation:

C'est un grand garçon maigre, pâle au visage imberbe éclairé par deux yeux d'une extrême vivacité ... Il a la parole facile et se défend avec une âpreté qui décèle d'incontestables qualités d'énergie et de ténacité... Il a su défendre ses positions avec une surprenante énergie, réfutant tous les points de l'instruction.[2]

And similarly upon his return to France his verbal genius was remarked upon both in the meetings in Halévy's *salon* and during the colloquia at Pontigny where, according to information gleaned by that admirable biographer Jean Lacouture, "Il fait fureur."[3] Increasingly this talent was directed into more formal channels as Malraux became during the 1930s a sought-after speaker for many of the causes espoused by the National Front, culminating in his visits to Moscow, Germany, and North America.

It should perhaps be pointed out for the sake of completeness that there were occasional critics unconvinced *at that time* of Malraux's authentic talent as an orator. François Mauriac considered, for example, that his prodigious literary gifts limited the effectiveness of his public speaking:

Dès que Malraux ouvre la bouche, son magnétisme faiblit. Non qu'il n'y ait en lui de quoi faire un tribun, et même un grand tribun; mais le littérateur lui coupe le sifflet. Les images qu'il invente, au lieu de réchauffer son discours, le glacent: elles sont trop compliquées, on y sent la mise au point laborieuse de l'homme de lettres.[4]

But such an opinion would seem to be strongly challenged by the prevailing impression typified by one anecdote which emerged, in fact from his North American visit, and which was reported in *Commune* in 1937. At Montreal Malraux had noted, among the dollars and cheques that appeared in the collection for the Spanish Republican cause which had as usual followed his speech, a watch dated 1860. When the donor, an old workman, was identified to him, Malraux tells us that the following conversation ensued:

Pourquoi avez-vous mis votre montre? Je sais que vous êtes pauvre. Etes-vous des nôtres?
–Je ne connais rien à la politique, me répondit-il, mais sur l'Espagne il y a une chose que maintenant j'ai comprise. J'ai compris qu'il y avait des hommes, quelle que soit leur opinion politique, qui se battent actuellement pour qu'on puisse leur faire confiance. Et cette chose si simple est la chose la plus importante de ma vie et c'est pour ça que j'ai mis dans le plateau pour l'Espagne la seule chose que je possédais, celle à laquelle j'attachais le plus d'importance.[5]

The man of letters had reached the man of no letters, and at the most visceral level.

However, it was really after World War II, in the cause of Gaullism, that Malraux's oratorical powers were first utilized on a regular basis, as he became the principal herald and spokesman for the General. It was during this period which, apart from the temporary withdrawal in the fifties, extended right up to de Gaulle's death, that Malraux rose on so many occasions to prepare the way so effectively for him. Often with nothing more in writing than a few choice sentences, and a slogan as *leitmotif*, he succeeded almost unfailingly in inducing that semi-hypnotic trance which characterized these public performances. Claude Mauriac bore witness thus in 1948:

Je conserverai du congrès R.P.F. de Marseille le souvenir inoubliable de la séance de clôture, le samedi 17, au Palais Chanot, où prirent la parole Malraux puis de Gaulle, d'une façon admirable l'un et l'autre, mais surtout le premier qui n'était jamais apparu aussi *grand*, dans le lyrisme politique et la poésie historique (quelles images! et quel ton!) envoûtant la foule par les sortilèges d'un rythme verbal que double, à contretemps, le corps haletant.[6]

Indeed, few who have been fortunate enough to see or hear Malraux speak could fail to have been marked by that intense, almost chanted, delivery peculiar to Malraux throughout his life, and which consistently elevated the subject in question. Nevertheless it is worth noting that Malraux himself makes an interesting distinction between the improvised political speeches of this period and the polished funeral or celebrational orations which punctuated his final years.[7] He suggests that the former are immediately linked to a specific action, a desired goal, whereas the latter are really in all cases an ultimate consecration of a communion in the face of Death. Although undoubtedly there is much that is pertinent in this division, and I shall explore it more thoroughly in the body of this analysis, it should first be admitted that there does, nevertheless, seem to emerge from *any* Malraux speech a transcendental tone that attests the inevitable presence of the same mystical filter to be found in his fiction and essays.

It is my intention, therefore, in the following pages not only to attempt to determine the specific characteristics of Malraux's oratory, but also to investigate in what ways these differ from, repeat, or illuminate those that are considered to be typical of his literature.

What can be in no doubt from the outset is that Malraux himself was very aware of the technique of public speaking in all its aspects – structural, psychological, material, and other. Certainly he reveals in both his novelistic and autobiographical writings a keen observation of the least nuances of any speaker's art. Mao, for example, is admired as early as *Les Conquérants* for his ability to influence a crowd through a combination of posture, tone, and vocabulary.[8] In *La Condition humaine*, through the mouth of Vologuine, it is to Lenin that Malraux pays homage, applauding the Russian's capacity and determination to lead a listener through complex ideas to an ever more enlightened understanding: "Les discours de Lénine, ces spirales opiniâtres par lesquelles il revenait six fois sur le même point, un étage plus haut chaque fois."[9] On yet another occasion it is the speeches of Nehru which have come under close scrutiny:

Certains discours de Nehru, surtout les discours de combat, étaient des discours d'orateur au sens traditionnel, par l'organisation de la persuasion, par l'éloquence. Mais nombre de ses discours aux masses ressemblaient à de longs monologues, et il les prononçait presque sur le ton de la conversation.[10]

Even as late as 1966 Malraux remains extremely attentive to the subtleties of oral delivery. While attending an exhibition of African sculpture at Dakar, Malraux discovers in Senghor's speech, perhaps with a certain tacit empathy, some of those difficulties of changing medium that must be encountered by any essentially literary person turned orator: "Quelques-unes de ses formules sont très élaborées, parce qu'ils les a écrites autrefois, et reprises dans son discours d'inauguration."[11]

This longstanding attention paid to the craft of the public speaker was clearly not gratuitous, for the lessons to be learned were necessarily relevant to Malraux's own oral performance. And there is no doubt that Malraux was not only enormously concerned with the content and delivery of his speeches, but even took considerable care over the minute technical details. On one occasion in Guyana, for example, his preoccupation with the precise physical circumstance that is involved in any public utterance is far greater than that of the prefect whose responsibility, in fact, the occasion was: "Nous [le préfet et Malraux] parlâmes de l'organisation du discours, que je devrais prononcer quelques heures plus tard. Ou plutôt je parlais organisation, micros, service d'ordre, situation politique; et il me répondait cérémonies."[12]

Nor did Malraux's perfectionism in this regard cease at the point where the speech itself was concluded, for he was equally rigorous with regard to any subsequent re-transmission. Brigitte Friang reveals in her account of Malraux the intensity of his annoyance with regard to the quality of one recording which had been broadcast. He deplored, we are told, "Cette reproduction sur les ondes, qui magnifiait impitoyablement et parfois jusqu'à l'insupportable, le côté déclamatoire de ses envolées."[13]

Despite Malraux's evident awareness of the overall specificity of oratory, this passion for order and perfection is obviously closely related to the one which Julien Green, among others, had already noticed with regard to Malraux's composition of his novels.[14] And undoubtedly there are profound similarities between his oral and written modes of expression. In both one discovers, for example, the use of ellipsis, the telescoping of ideas, a fractured rhythm that rejects the reasonableness of syntax. In both too there is often a common elevated level of expression that integrates vibrant pleas and lyrical flights. However, while recognizing that an epic tone prevails almost throughout, I would not care to subscribe further to the unusually sardonic assessment of Professor Frohock when he considers Malraux's speech at Athens on the occasion of the opening of the illuminations of the Acropolis: "One wonders how the night when he pushed a switch in the name of General de Gaulle for the Philips Radio Company could become fateful enough to sing about."[15] The answer to this laconic query would seem to be explicit in Malraux's own account of the event in *La Corde et les souris*: "Le gouvernement hellénique m'avait invité pour la première illumination de l'Acropole ... J'apportais aux combattants grecs de la Résistance, l'hommage des nôtres."[16] Surely, given Malraux's scheme of things, nothing could be more liable to activate his sense of the epic than a situation where he was charged with communicating a human solidarity which transcended space and time, in a setting that was itself so fraught with human and cultural resonance. A measured perspective would recognize that Malraux frequently penetrates the logical surface of an event or a situation, and emerges onto a level which is akin to the mystical. In this way the *apparently* banal indeed is invested with meaning and magic, but by a Malraux who is a visionary rather than an ingenious counterfeiter. William Righter, in an important essay on the rhetorical quality of Malraux's writings, and with particular reference to the period dominated by the latter's essays on art, seems to hold a similar opinion:

In *Les Noyers de l'Altenburg* Malraux speaks of the special genius of the shaman – whose kind of magic survives in our world largely through the great artist. Without forcing an artificial comparison there is no doubt that Malraux regards his task in his aesthetic writings not only as closer to art than to academic historical study, but to a special kind of art which combines that urgency of the prophet's message with the rhetorical apparatus and eloquence of the great preachers. He intends not to demonstrate but to illumine, and seeks not the ordinary sort of intellectual conviction, but something akin to conversion. To illuminate, to transform, to excite, to inflame – these are the aims of the sudden juxtapositions, the dazzling comparisons, the acrobatic play of words and images. Malraux presents himself in the double role of the seer, the visionary – and of the orator, in whose passionate verbal display a revolutionary spirit has lost none of its fervour.[17]

But despite this proximity of tone in Malraux the novelist and Malraux the orator, there are also, of course, fundamental distinctions to be made, at least in passing. It may well be, for example, that the immediate and ephemeral nature of the speaker/audience contact requires the speaker to be more emphatic and affirmative than the writer who, given the reader's possibility of recall, can remain at the level of the interrogative, or even the enigmatic. Similarly, comparative analysis of related content tends to suggest that Malraux makes more effort in his speeches to render his material digestible by a largely non-intellectual audience – far more so anyway than in his imaginative writings, of which he has adamantly asserted: "Je n'écris pas pour m'embêter!"[18] Such distinctions, however, are more likely to prove instructive at the level of the mediums themselves than with special reference to Malraux.

In attempting to find suitable categories under which to examine more closely Malraux's actual speeches, the more traditional frames of reference do not seem particularly useful. The title that Malraux himself attached to his 1971 volume of collected speeches, *Oraisons funèbres*, invites us obviously to consider Bossuet's organization of a speech into *texte, exorde, partie centrale, péroraison*, but such a formal strait-jacket does not satisfactorily contain any of Malraux's speeches that I have examined. Indeed, even Bossuet himself finished by denouncing such an excessively ceremonial conception, in fact terming it profane. Nor do Aristotle's labels of *political, judicial, epideictic* advance us very far. Rather it is to Etienne Fuzellier's remarks on eloquence in his incisive little book *Cinéma et littérature* that I am indebted for the simple, but I believe useful, division that sustains my analysis. Fuzellier argues that the orator is seeking to communicate a certain "état d'âme," one that necessarily embraces a state of mind *and* a state of sensibility, one that seeks to operate at the level of reason as well as the level of emotion.[19] There is, therefore, a demonstrative and logical component, an arranged argument, which seeks to persuade; there is also an affective component which attempts to achieve an almost incantatory, hypnotic, complicity by the use of a selection of devices which may include tone, rhythm, body, orchestration. With regard to Malraux, although these components are both present in most of his speeches, he seems to lean significantly to one or the other on any single occasion. In other words, and while recognizing the clear limit of such a classification, it does seem possible to consider Malraux's speeches as characterized essentially either by a tendency towards *persuasion*, or else by a tendency towards *communion*.[20]

It is perhaps symptomatic of the importance which Malraux attaches to persuasive oratory that both the first and the last of his novelistic heroes are active in the organization of propaganda. Garine, in *Les Conquérants*, is "chargé de la direction générale de la propagande" in Canton,[21] and Vincent Berger in *Les Noyers de l'Altenburg* was employed in his early years as Director of Propaganda for the German Embassy in Turkey. Moreover, evidence once more of that peculiar imaginative anticipation of a real event that often characterized his life, Malraux himself was initially to achieve ministerial status in Information. The potentiality to persuade could reasonably be posited as the common driving force in each of these experiences.

It is once more to Garine that we turn for the first, more precise, indication of the nature of the persuasive craft. We discover in his advice to Lo Moi that he attaches great importance to the need to focus the listener's attention on something solid and clear, perhaps an object or a symbol:

Dans les derniers déclenchements de grève, à Hong-Kong et ici, trop de discours inutiles. Si les camarades se croient dans un Parlement, ils se trompent! Et, une fois pour toutes, ces discours-là doivent être soutenus par un objet: si la maison du patron est trop loin, ou si elle est trop moche, ils peuvent toujours avoir son auto sous la main. Je répète, pour la dernière fois, que les orateurs doivent montrer ce qu'ils attaquent.[22]

Garine's forceful remonstration[23] calls to mind the explanation given in *Les Noyers de l'Altenburg* concerning Vincent Berger's effectiveness in Turkish. It is the latter's spontaneous packaging of simple, concrete ideas which is striking in a language not normally so direct in its expressions: "l'éloquence tendue du professeur Vincent Berger, d'autant plus frappante qu'en turc elle remplaçait par des slogans les arabesques traditionnelles."[24]

Perhaps another means by which an audience can be provided with something accessible, onto which it can fasten, is the anecdote. This recourse to a story imbued not only with historical truth, but with people and places that are recognizable and, to some degree, familiar, provides an initial point of communication, a bridge which will eventually facilitate the passing of the message. An excellent example of such a device is to be found in Malraux's 1965 speech concerning de Gaulle and the Republic, on the occasion of the second round of voting in the presidential elections. The story Malraux includes recounts a moment during his previous visit as de Gaulle's representative to Mexico. During a conversation with a Mexican teacher in the Puebla museum, Malraux had been struck by the apparent incongruity of the Mexican's evident warmth towards France and the fact that they were standing in front of a group of frescoes which represented the combat between the French and the Mexican Revolutionary Army. When he commented on this, he was informed by the teacher that Mexican children begin their French by learning just a few set expressions, one of which is a sentence taken from a letter sent by Victor Hugo to President Juarès just prior to Maximilian's victory: "Si vous devenez vainqueur, Monsieur le Président, vous trouverez chez moi l'hospitalité du citoyen, si vous êtes vaincu, vous y trouverez l'hospitalité du proscrit."[25] Malraux further stimulates the curiosity of his audience by stressing that here we have a sentence learned by heart by every Mexican child, but almost totally unknown among their French counterparts. France, for Mexico, *is* this letter, confirms Malraux's humble teacher. Malraux, having captured his audience with this delightful revelation, is not slow to conclude that in such a historic context only de Gaulle, known throughout South and Central America as *libertador*, is a worthy leader of France.

Indeed, the anecdote just considered leads into a passage characterized by the extensive use of another technique by which a point of view can effectively be transmitted – humour, on this occasion of a particularly lacerating variety in which the unfortunate victim is the present incumbent of the French presidency.[26] Mitterand was at that time leader of the self-styled "Union des républicains," in opposition to de Gaulle, against therefore, Malraux points out ironically, a man "qui a sauvé deux fois la République." A lengthy enumeration of de Gaulle's substantial achievements as the true defender of liberty in France is contrasted with a flat declaration of the patent inadequacy of Mitterand and his associates: "Vous avez *rêvé* la Gauche! Vous croyez que vous la faites quand vous parlez d'elle." Malraux goes further and, with a sarcasm to which the crowd hastens to respond, he encapsulates the absurdity of Mitterand's position in a single, witheringly memorable sentence: "Vous êtes le candidat unique de quatre Gauches, dont l'extrême Droite!"

A gift for trenchant aphorism is borne out by the subsequent juxtaposition of the "pouvoir personnel" of de Gaulle and the "impuissance impersonnelle" of his electoral opponent; a penchant for caricature when he reduces Mitterand's much-vaunted humility to "ce merveilleux air de virginité politique et de modeste hauteur." Humour, as a weapon on behalf of a cause, is far from being new. Although he uses it sparingly, there can no doubt as to its presence, its purpose, and its ravaging potency in Malraux's political speeches.

Perhaps it would be as well at this point to provide historical evidence of Malraux's effectiveness as a *persuasive* speaker.[27] One of the key moments, not only of his own political development, but also in the early post-war evolution of French political life, was undoubtedly the MLN Congress at the Mutualité in January 1945. The Congress had been split during most of its proceedings into two fundamentally irreconcilable attitudes; the one favoured a fusion with the National

Front, the other was opposed to such a fusion. With no solution in sight, it was on the third day that Malraux took the microphone. He is described thus by Jean Lacouture:

Voici Malraux, dressé encore une fois sur cette tribune où il a défendu Thaelmann, Dimitrov et une République espagnole dominée (en 1938) par les communistes. Vareuse khaki à cinq galons, baudrier, bottes de cheval. Il est très pâle et, note le reporter de *Combat*... "animé de la même passion avec laquelle il commande sur le front la brigade Alsace-Lorraine." Il se prend alors pour Saint-Just et Hoche à la fois et lance de sa voix de crépuscule...[28]

The result is conclusive. He succeeds by a concerted combination of passion and persuasive device in convincing a solid majority to reject the proposed unification: "Il est très applaudi. C'est son intervention qui porte le coup de grâce aux champions de l'unification."[29]

At no time, however, were Malraux's talents in this direction more evident than when he was presenting the leader for whom he felt such unbounded admiration. Indeed, even when he was not actually speaking himself, Malraux concerned himself with the organization of those spectacles, those ceremonial "happenings" that were so often advantageous to de Gaulle's cause. Through Malraux's awareness of motivating factors and attention to technical detail, when Charles de Gaulle rose to speak during those heady days of the RPF much of the conditioning had already been done; the audience was utterly receptive. Once again it is to Jean Lacouture that we are indebted for an account:

Trois années durant, Charles de Gaulle fut un immense druide gaulois opposant aux Tartares et aux ilotes du système une haute silhouette éclairée et une grande voix sonorisée par les soins du cinéaste de *L'Espoir*. Musique, lumières, plans d'eau, foules dans la pénombre criant leur attente et leur colère, podiums drapés de tricolore et balcons surplombant les masses houleuses, services d'ordre musclés et slogans sommaires, tout fut fait pour que le grand cérémonial revêtit le caractère sacré, militant et sonore qui permet de mettre les foules en condition et de tirer d'elles le rendement le plus intense.[30]

As the above passage attests, it would be naïve to contend that the tentative line I have drawn between the speeches primarily of persuasion and those that seek communion is always a clear one. Rather, especially where de Gaulle is concerned, the question of whether it is political commitment or mystical complicity which predominates for Malraux is a particularly complex one. Certainly, at the time of de Gaulle's return to power, for example at the Hôtel de Ville in Paris in July 1958,[31] the psychological platform prepared by Malraux's introductory speech has taken on the awesome overtones of the pulpit. By a series of intentionally dazzling leaps of time and space Malraux weaves a pattern of world history and legend in which de Gaulle appears as the central figure. With the accent placed decisively, and with superb simplicity, on little more than the word "Non," presented as the verbal token of resistance to all that seeks to degrade Man, Malraux achieves a miraculous symbiosis. One which not only embraces the Free French and the Maquis, but situates de Gaulle firmly alongside Jeanne d'Arc, Antigone, and Prometheus! The result of such an evocation of much of that which is most resonant in both history and myth is to create an atmosphere that smacks more of a religious celebration than a political harangue.

A similar elegant mystification is evident in Malraux's speech on the draft constitution in September of that same year.[32] Having prepared the way once more with a vocabulary highly charged with epic overtones, Malraux provides a climax by linking with delightful succinctness de Gaulle's past, unimpeachable, and heroic action to his present, political stance: "Ici Londres. Les Français parlent aux Français. Vous allez entendre le Général de Gaulle." The unforgettable wartime announcement that symbolized for so many Frenchmen the survival of hope and patriotism is first powerfully recalled verbatim by Malraux. It then becomes, and in precisely the same tone, "Ici *Paris* etc., etc." A single word is changed, a mere geographic variation, as the listeners, entrapped at a visceral level, are urged subliminally to regard the two situations as identical, and de Gaulle once again as the saviour.

Even if, on occasion, there does seem to be a great deal of similarity between some of the techniques used to achieve persuasion and those designed to conjure up communion, there is of course one important distinction. Although in both cases Malraux may choose to call, for example, on a certain hypnotic frame of reference, one that is beguilingly prestigious, invoking characteristically war, resistance, ancestors, destiny, fraternity, and hope, there does remain an essential difference with regard to the self-interest of the speaker. For, in its purest form, when there is no political motive, such a frame of reference has no other objective than to encompass listener and speaker in the complicity of a very special experience. There can be few orators of the twentieth century who have sought and accomplished such a state of entranced communion as that which was engendered by the most remarkable of Malraux's performances. It is to these speeches that I shall now turn.

As Garine pointed out in *Les Conquérants*, repeated, brief allusions to an object, a slogan, or a formula are particularly useful in directing the listeners' attention and in realizing by accumulation the desired persuasion. But, in certain circumstances, such repetition is also liable to be incantatory and, thereby, contribute to that mystical communion we are examining. The black-robed womenfolk of Corrèze and the shadowy heroes of the Resistance are used as recurrent, resonant, images in this way on more than one occasion in Malraux's speeches. What they represent is a refusal to succumb, to submit, a glorious force which stands fast against fatality in whatever form and steadfastly says "Non!" Indeed, here in the most distilled form it is this single vibrant syllable, referred to earlier in a different context, which stands for Malraux as an authentic sign of all that is heroic in mankind in firm opposition to the servility of "Ceux qui disent oui."[33] It is this "Non," as both refrain and motto, which punctuates at Athens Malraux's spoken veneration of the legacy of Greece: "Le seul peuple qui célèbre une fête du 'Non'."[34] At Glières it is with a litany of "Non" that Malraux reveres the "maquisard":

Toutes les plus hautes figures spirituelles de l'humanité ont dit Non à César. Prométhée règne sur la tragédie et sur notre mémoire pour avoir dit Non aux Dieux ... Ce non du maquisard obscur collé à la terre pour sa première nuit de mort, suffit à faire de ce pauvre gars le compagnon de Jeanne et d'Antigone.[35]

If "Non" is the ultimate verbal image of man's courage, undiminished through history, then it has an evocatory capacity situated at the most vital level. Both symbol and psalm, its repeated utterance cannot fail to reanimate what, in Jungian terms, must be an important attribute of our collective unconscious, and to stimulate a complicity that is indeed profound.

A further key to the consistency of Malraux's priorities in speeches of this type is offered by analysis of divergencies between the original written version of a speech (or its *post facto* published form) and the actual oral delivery. In nearly every case any substantive change can be reasonably explained by the speaker's desire to emphasize the sense of comradeship that needed to prevail for the event to be successful. It may be, for example, a single word that is changed. Thus, in a speech in 1964 commemorating the death of Joan of Arc, "fraternelle" displaces "affectueuse," the latter appearing in the written text:

Nous connaissons tous son supplice. Mais les mêmes textes qui peu à peu dégagent de la légende son image véritable, son rêve, ses pleurs, l'efficace et fraternelle (affectueuse) autorité qu'elle partage avec les fondatrices d'ordres religieux, ces mêmes textes dégagent aussi, de son supplice, deux des moments les plus pathétiques de l'histoire de la douleur.[36]

Elsewhere too, "fraternel" recurs instead of words that appear relatively colourless, constituting a persistent appeal, instinctive perhaps, to twentieth-century man's yearning for some means by which to combat his essential and anguished solitude. On at least one occasion, at the Panthéon at the time of the transfer of Jean Moulin's ashes, Malraux inserts into his projected speech an entirely new explicative sentence concerning fraternity that is only marginally linked with the immediate context: "Ce sentiment qui appelle la légende, sans lequel la Résistance n'eût existé, et qui nous réunit aujourd'hui, c'est peut-être simplement l'accent invisible de la fraternité."[37] Such departures from the rigour with which Malraux customarily adhered to his prepared text on ceremonial occasions would seem to be rare and always revealing.[38] Another instance occurs earlier in the same speech when a considerable passage, scheduled to be delivered in the third person, becomes in fact transposed into the intimacy of the second person singular. This change, in the heat of the moment so to speak, is perhaps even more symptomatic than the clear preponderance in Malraux's oratory, as opposed to his literature, of second and first person pronouns, which tend to embrace listener, speaker, and very often subject, into a single collectivity.[39] Even, on occasion, extending dramatically to include those absent or dead in a revival of the prosopopoeia of ancient rhetoric.

Of course, it is self-evident that by definition speaking is normally an experience presupposing immediate communication, whereas writing is not. In other words, Malraux the orator, with the advantage of contact, is inevitably better placed to instil an awareness of human solidarity than Malraux the writer. However, it is worth recalling that Malraux does make use, in those speeches I have designated as of "communion," of techniques that are to be found just as readily in his literature. One could cite, for instance, a carefully linear progression which leads from the prosaic conviction of facts and dates to the emotional thrust that demands to be shared. Or the structure may be a circular one, one that is mystical by definition according to commentators like d'Annunzio and Jakobsen. Perfect in shape, returning ineluctably to its point of departure, such is the chosen organization of Malraux's speech at the Louvre in September 1965 during the funeral of Le Corbusier. Beginning with the telegram from the Greek architects announcing their funeral gift of earth from the

Acropolis, and a second one from India, offering water from the Ganges, the speech continues through the gamut of Le Corbusier's accomplishments before returning in the final words to the gifts alluded to in the initial telegrams: "Adieu, mon vieux maître et mon vieil ami ... Voici l'eau sacrée du Gange et la terre de l'Acropole."[40] The structure – A, B, corpus, B, A – is indeed a perfect circle, image of the completed curve of human life, our common fate. Not only are we embraced in the ritual harmony of the moment, but also in the absoluteness of this dreadful finality. However, such deliberate devices may be less productive with regard to the ear than they are to the eye, the possibility of recall in literature being more available than in discourse. In fact, not only need the organization of a speech not be formally literary, it may scarcely exist at all. As Malraux recognizes in *Le Temps du mépris*, emotion can be shared despite, perhaps even because of, an inherent and dominant awkwardness in the speaker: "Tous étaient avec elle; sa maladresse avait été la leur et tandis qu'elle reculait vers le fond de la tribune, les applaudissements secourables montaient vers elle comme sa douleur avait été vers eux."[41]

Similarly, Malraux recognizes that the flattest of deliveries can be effective and may even generate a state that almost seems to transcend reality – witness the magic of Gandhi: "Un jour ... il parlait devant quelques centaines de milliers de personnes, de sa voix égale de baryton, avec un micro. Dans une clairière, entre de grands arbres fleuris, des frangipaniers, je crois... Les fleurs se sont mises à tomber." [42] Malraux himself, of course, was far removed from such evenness of tone. Much more likely was a dramatic emphasis on a particular sound. Thus, at a key moment in his speech commemorating the death of Joan of Arc, the clearly prolonged vibrancy of a series or "r" sounds turns a known historical fact into a triumphant, gutteral, cry: "le sacr-r-re qui r-rétablit le r-roi!"[43] Elsewhere in the same speech we discover the unnatural but effective extension of a vowel to convey tension, followed immediately by the abrupt "vint" that marks the onset of Joan's physical agony: "Et la première fla-a-amme vint."

There is little to suggest that such phonetic effects were necessarily "artful." On the contrary, there exist several testimonies which rather reveal the extraordinary degree to which the Malraux of the podium, in a moment of communion with the crowd before him, far more than a craftsman, was a man entranced. Brigitte Friang notes: "Malraux entrait dans un état second lorsqu'il parlait en public."[44] Even more informative is her anecdote which gives Malraux's reply when asked what he had said at the beginning of a particular speech: "Ce que j'ai dit au début ... mais comment voulez-vous que je m'en souvienne?"[45] As Brigitte Friang points out herself: "Lorsque l'on jouissait d'une mémoire aussi fantastique que la sienne, la réponse était significative."

As I suggested earlier, even those speeches which commence with an apparently cold and logical rigour soon shift onto another plane. Thus the orations for Jean Moulin and Joan of Arc, initially chronicles, are, when the speaker proceeds to evoke the time of torture and sacrifice, increasingly punctuated by sobs of emotion as the affectivity takes charge. Nor is there any doubt that on most occasions this emotion communicates itself to the gathered crowd and leads all towards one final and shared *cry*.

Indeed, in the most remarkable of instances so climactic is the experience that all discourse halts and a less banal vehicle takes over. It is then that total communion becomes manifest in an all-subsuming music.

Although critics have, perhaps erroneously, insisted on more than one occasion on Malraux's limitations with regard to musical appreciation, few would refuse to aknowledge a definite rhythmic presence in both his literary and his oral expression. Be it on account of the balance and structure of individual phrases and sentences, or the composition of a group of sentences – and regardless of largely unfruitful questions of intentionality – the reiterated critical designations of "psalmodie," "mélopée," "chant," and "cantate" are undoubtedly justified. Certainly Malraux himself was convinced that speeches are fundamentally "liés au rythme de la voix."[46] Rachel Bespaloff, one of the most perceptive of those who took an early interest in Malraux, goes still further in a suggestion dating from 1938: "Il y a toujours chez Malraux ... cet instant où l'intelligence fourbue, à bout de mots, s'abandonne à la musique."[47] And there is no doubt that that intinerary proposed by Rachel Bespaloff is evident in certain of Malraux's communion speeches as the rhythm of the intelligent voice becomes, in the moment of climax, not only a cry, but a hymn.

Two examples of the way in which musicality can ensure that rite of passage by which speaker and audience become fused into a single entity, a veritable microcosm of mankind, are to be found in the speeches Malraux made on a visit to the Caribbean on behalf of de Gaulle. Referring to Guadeloupe, Malraux acknowledges the inherent susceptibility of that particular audience to a solidarity generated in this way: "Je parlais pour la première fois devant une foule noire et je sentais son immobilité frémissante s'accorder au rythme du discours comme sa danse s'accorde à la musique."[48] And in Martinique, speaking after Aimé Césaire, Malraux allows his final stirring sentences to merge into the solemn initial bars of the "Marseillaise," before the explosion of "Aux armes, citoyens!" Even beyond a frenetically passionate salutation to the absent, legendary General, Malraux sees in this shared experience, once again, a sacred reaffirmation of human fraternity: "C'était le hurlement de la liberté noire, celui des combattants de Toussaint Louverture et de l'éternelle Jacquerie-inextricablement mêlé à l'espoir révolutionnaire, à la fraternité physique."[49]

Although emphatic, such experiences are, of course, not in any way confined to those who by tradition enjoy a natural sensitivity to rhythm. The passage from spoken word to bells at the end of Malraux's speech on 24 August 1958 celebrating the anniversary of the liberation of Paris is not at all dissimilar to those detailed above.[50] However, it may well be that the most extraordinary concerting of discourse and music occurs in the Jean Moulin speech to which I have already alluded.

The scene itself on that remarkable day is unforgettably recalled by Jean Lacouture:

Il fait très froid rue Soufflot. Le général de Gaulle est là, immense dans l'immense capote de campagne qui l'enveloppe jusqu'aux pieds, comme au temps de la bataille des Ardennes. Malraux s'est avancé sur l'esplanade énorme, jusqu'au pupitre et au micro, d'un pas d'automate épuisé. Il grippe comme une bouée les feuillets de son discours. Sa voix brisée flotte sur le vent de glace comme un noyé ballotté par les vagues.[51]

Towards the end of the speech, in which skilful rhetoric and controlled intensity have already established a rhythm that is almost a chant, a drum begins to add further weight and resonance to the words. The very first beat underscores heavily in Malraux's discourse the decisive word "complicité," the second "psalmodier." It is probably unnecessary to stress the significance of these two "chosen" words for the present study! With supreme effect, both drumbeat and spoken word give way finally, but with no hiatus, to the moving "Chant des partisans" as Malraux concludes, with a hoarseness that is almost inhuman, on the collectivity "France."[52]

Such an arrangement, beyond confirming the attention to detail and orchestration that does seem to characterize Malraux's finest oral efforts, leaves one in no doubt as to the primacy of a communion achieved through ritual and rhythm. The result on occasions like the one I have just examined, surely one of the highpoints of celebrational oratory in this century, is a state of hypnotic participation in which circumstance and utterance are transcended by an enduring human kinship. What we are dealing with, although divorced from any religious support, is not dissimilar to the sharing of wine and bread in the holy office. Or, in purely human terms, and perhaps with greater relevance in the case of Malraux, such speeches may be viewed not as mere discourse, but as a further example of those *situations extrêmes* which Malraux sought throughout his life. Once again a passage from *Le Temps du mépris* seems to offer confirmation:

il [le nouvel orateur] retrouvait les passions et les vérités qui ne sont données qu'aux hommes assemblés. C'était la même exaltation qu'à l'envol des escadrilles de guerre, lorsque l'avion fonçait pour le départ entre deux autres, pilotes et observateurs braqués vers le même combat. Et toute cette communion à la fois ahurie, grave et farouche où il commençait à se retrouver.[53]

Only in the long shadow of Death, in a situation characterized by such aggrandizement and intensity, does man approach an absolute; only then do notions of self-affirmation, domination, and above all fraternity, have any real value. Far more of course than any literature, such are the principal experiences of Malraux's adventurous life. Such, in the final analysis, is his – and perhaps our – experience of oratory.

Conclusion

"Comprendre une œuvre" n'est pas une
expression moins confuse que "comprendre
un homme." Il ne s'agit pas de rendre
une œuvre intelligible, mais de rendre
sensible à ce qui fait sa valeur.
(Malraux, *L'Homme précaire et la
littérature*, 14)

It is relatively banal to observe in general terms that creative art in the twentieth century poses more questions than it answers. But such a statement does nevertheless offer very real illumination when it is applied to the writings of André Malraux; for, in his work, increasingly, as his early concerns for immediacy are better integrated, particularly in the light of the *Sierra de Teruel* experience, an interrogative mode is fashioned to inform with ever greater coherence an interrogative exploration of the nature of transcendence in a dreadfully human twentieth century.

Of course, Malraux himself recognizes clearly the fundamentally disruptive challenge held out by an artist: "la création bouleverse plus qu'elle ne perfectionne," and in particular by a great artist – here the novelist: "peut-être tenons-nous pour grand tout roman qui atteint à l'interrogation."[1] Nor is there any doubt that this corresponds closely to Malraux's conception of his own work and its principal preoccupation: "L'interrogation métaphysique joue dans mon œuvre le rôle capital."[2] Moreover, Malraux's predilection for "interrogation," which presupposes a rejection of the primacy of rigid expression or affirmation, is reinforced by his theory of metamorphosis, present figuratively in his final novel, but enunciated with particular frequency and clarity in his later years: "Ma réponse à Spengler, c'est une théorie de la métaphorphose; dans le domaine de l'art, et dans celui de la pensée. L'essentiel d'une grande pensée, c'est sa puissance de métamorphose."[3]

Undoubtedly the key work in this regard, and the one which establishes theoretically Malraux's final position as to what really characterizes twentieth-century man and his civilization, is *L'Homme précaire et la littérature*, published posthumously in 1977. In that work Malraux states unequivocally the invertebrate, amorphous, provisional nature of our world in terms which go beyond the Absurd to the *aleatory*: "Devant l'aléatoire, ni le monde ni l'homme n'ont de sens, puisque sa définition même est l'impossibilité d'un sens," and the *precarious*: "avec autant de rigueur que la chrétienté enfanta le chrétien, la plus puissante civilisation de l'histoire aura enfanté l'homme précaire."[4]

Against such a tenuous, shifting, unsubstantial background in recent years, and without reiterating the earlier qualitative changes which take place between the *écrits farfelus* and the mature novels, it seems curious that some critics would still choose to see Malraux's writings as in any way static or easy to circumscribe. More than one critic has maintained, for example, that most of what Malraux has to say is probably present as early as 1926 in the essay "D'une jeunesse européenne," and is certainly present by the time of *La Condition humaine*; or, similarly, that the latter volume is without doubt the culmination of Malraux's creative activity. Such charges would make Malraux intellectually and artistically bankrupt at thirty-two years of age! It is to be hoped that the preceding pages may have helped to demonstrate that such is not the case, neither with regard to his ideas nor his style.

Inevitably, in a world that is languishing in the spectral shadow of Death, there are indeed certain constants: a yearning for some fraternity to combat man's essential solitude, a refusal to sink without effort into the vortex of the Absurd, a conviction that life is to be lived, fully and intensely – these undoubtedly recur. The human condition is what it is, and certain persistent human reactions do remain. But beyond that, the nuances are considerable. Certainly, the way in which Malraux's man, and of course Malraux, cope with their condition does seem to reveal a definite evolution. From playful adolescence the reader follows Malraux through the dichotomy of anguish and glorification in his middle years, towards the entirely "provisional" utterances of the mature man. The often frivolous, sometimes sardonic, humour of youth is but a temporary shield against a painful recognition of the abyss, prior to the discovery of a very tentative equilibrium in the philosophy of metamorphosis and the aleatory espoused more vigorously by an older Malraux. At the time of "D'une jeunesse européenne" the predominant attitude was one of incomprehension, deprivation, and frustration:

Il semble que notre civilisation tende à se créer une métaphysique d'où tout but fixe soit exclu, du même ordre que sa conception de la matière. L'Homme et le Moi l'un après l'autre détruits, que peut une telle métaphysique contre les besoins de l'âme?

A quel destin est donc vouée cette jeunesse violente, merveilleusement armée contre elle-même, et délivrée de la basse vanité de nommer grandeur le dédain d'une vie à laquelle elle ne sait pas se lier?[5]

But, by the 1950s, that tortured "question" has already become its own accepted mode of existence. No longer wracked by his *Angst*, the mature Malraux discerns and then embraces the interrogative itself as the only valid human attitude: "Notre civilisation ... se fonde sur des questions."[6]

Necessarily his narrative technique is determined by this same evolution, and it is that conviction which has coloured, without overly concerting, all of the preceding chapters. Indeed I would go so far as to assert that any essentially synchronic approach must surely be handicapped in its ability to illuminate a writer as clearly and as wilfully open to change and metamorphosis as Malraux. Only careful examination of the *changing* manifestations of Malraux's world, of *shifts* in artistic emphasis, of *modifications* in narrative form, can furnish adequate information about either his creative art or, ultimately, his vision of the world.

But even then – and, let it be said, while eschewing hagiography masquerading as criticism, I make no apology for an intense admiration with regard to Malraux – such is the richness of our subject that, however carefully considered the critical apparatus, however apposite the concept of the "colloque" to our times, however diligent the search, it would be excessively bold, as well as unsympathetic and inappropriate, to conclude any more positively than does Malraux himself!

Ce que j'ai écrit est plus important comme question que comme réponse. C'est vrai pour beaucoup d'écrivains, c'est vrai pour les philosophes.[7]

May it also be true for the critic.

Notes

INTRODUCTION

1 André Malraux, "Néocritique," in *Malraux: être et dire*, edited by M. de Courcel (Paris: Plon 1975), 297.
2 Lucien Goldmann, *Pour une sociologie du roman* (Paris: Gallimard 1970).
3 Malraux, "Néocritique," 307.

ON "LE MIROIR DES LIMBES"

1 In *Scènes choisies* (Paris: Gallimard 1946), 141.
2 See J.-M. Royer, "Malraux au piquet," *Le Point*, 27 Oct. 1975.
3 J. Lacouture, "Le Biographe et sa cible," *Le Magazine littéraire* (Sept. 1973): 34.
4 In an interview with Michel Droit, *Le Figaro littéraire*, 2 Oct. 1967.
5 André Malraux, *La Corde et les souris* (Paris: Gallimard 1976), 463.
6 André Malraux, *Antimémoires* (Paris: Gallimard 1972), exergual.
7 Ibid., 9.
8 Ibid., 19.
9 André Malraux, *Les Chênes qu'on abat* (Paris: Gallimard 1971), 7.
10 Ibid., 65. I return to this question more fully in chapter 5.
11 Ibid., 256.
12 Ibid., 371.
13 Malraux, *La Corde et les souris*, 166.
14 Malraux, *Antimémoires*, 555, 562.
15 Ibid., 377; Malraux, *La Corde et les souris*, 287.
16 In an interview with André Brincourt, *Le Figaro littéraire*, 30 Apr. 1971.

17 P.-H. Simon, "*Oraisons funèbres* d'André Malraux," *Le Monde des livres*, 13 Aug. 1971. See also chapter 11.
18 Claude Santelli in an interview in *La Croix*, 5 June 1972.
19 Ibid.
20 Ibid.
21 See note 4 above, 14.
22 See chapter 7.

ON THE PRESENT TENSE

1 From *Scènes choisies* (Paris: Gallimard 1946).
2 Julien Green, *Journal*, vol. 1, 1928–39 (Paris: Plon 1954), 26.
3 Malraux, "N'était-ce donc que cela?" *Liberté de l'esprit* (Apr. 1949): 9.
4 Malraux, *La Métamorphose des dieux* (Paris: Gallimard 1957), 1. The italics are Malraux's own.
5 Thomas Carlyle, *Histoire de la révolution française*, vol. 1, trans. E. Reynault and O. Barot (Paris: Baillière 1865), 252.
6 Raymond Radiguet, *Le Diable au corps* (Paris: Grasset 1971), 75.
7 Malraux, *Les Conquérants* (Paris: Grasset 1968), 11.
8 Malraux, *La Condition humaine* (Paris: Gallimard 1971), 7. The italics are mine.
9 Malraux, *Le Temps du mépris* (Paris: Gallimard 1945), 68.
10 Ibid., 70.
11 Although rarely noted, in terms of its tense variations, this passage is among the most remarkable of contemporary literature.
12 Only 47 out of 487 pages in Malraux, *L'Espoir* (Paris: Gallimard 1971).
13 Ibid., 397–8.
14 Ibid., 326.
15 Ibid., 253–4.
16 See Malraux, *Les Noyers de l'Altenburg* (Paris: Gallimard 1948). The last four paragraphs of the book are devoted decisively to this same theme, present of course more allusively since the evocation of the ancient but continuing forest of walnut trees in the title itself.

ON EROTICISM

1 Malraux, "Un chapitre inédit de *La Condition humaine*," *Marianne*, 13 Dec. 1933.
2 Malraux, *Lunes en papier* (Geneva: Skira 1945), 173.
3 For evident reasons of good taste there has been little publicity given to these blatantly erotic texts by the few researchers who are aware of their existence. However, one such volume, supervised by Malraux on behalf of the Kra publishing house, was on display at the exhibition of

"Malruciana" which accompanied the March 1978 International Conference on Malraux at Hofstra University, New York.

4 Malraux, *Les Conquérants*, 34.
5 Ibid., 148.
6 Malraux, *La Voie royale* (Paris: Grasset 1969), 9.
7 Ibid., 10.
8 Ibid., 157.
9 Malraux, "Préface," Lawrence, *L'Amant de Lady Chatterley* (Paris: Gallimard 1932), ii.
10 Ibid., iii.
11 Ibid.
12 Ibid., iii-iv.
13 Ibid., iv.
14 Elizbeth Tenenbaum, *The Problematic Self: Approaches to Identity in Stendhal, D.H. Lawrence and Malraux* (Cambridge: Harvard University Press 1977), vii.
15 W.H. Frohock, *André Malraux and the Tragic Imagination* (Stanford: Stanford University Press 1967), 75.
16 Malraux, *La Condition humaine*, 188.
17 D.H. Lawrence, *Lady Chatterley's Lover* (New York: New American Library 1959), 101.
18 Ibid., 219-20.
19 Anaïs Nin, *D.H. Lawrence: An Unprofessional Study* (Chicago: Swallow 1964), 109.
20 Malraux, *La Condition humaine*, 188. For a more developed study of this Tibetan symbol see chapter 6.
21 Ibid., 98.
22 Ibid., 99.
23 Ibid.
24 Ibid., 50.

ON FREE INDIRECT STYLE

1 (Paris: Gallimard 1977).
2 See Charles Bally, *Traité de stylistique française* (Geneva: Georg 1951). However, it was Professor Stephen Ullmann, at Leeds University in the 1960s, who first acquainted me with the multiple potentialities of free indirect style.
3 Malraux, *La Voie royale*, 128-9.
4 Malraux, *La Condition humaine*, 8-9.
5 Ibid., 53-4.
6 Malraux, *Le Temps du mépris*, 22-3.
7 This device was noted relatively late by linguists, probably only in the 1950s.

8 Malraux, *Le Temps du mépris*, 72–3.

9 Ibid., ix.

10 Quoted by André Vandegans, *La Jeunesse littéraire d'André Malraux* (Paris: Pauvert 1964).

11 Malraux writes in that preface, viii: "Le monde d'une oeuvre comme celle-ci, le monde de la tragédie ... se réduit à deux personnages, le héros et son sens de la vie."

12 See Jean Pouillon, *Temps et roman* (Paris: Gallimard 1946), chapter 2.

13 See chapter 2. It is also worth noting that other, similar, examples occur on pp. 91, 349, 350 of *L'Espoir*.

14 Malraux, *Les Noyers de l'Altenburg*, 214.

ON THE COMIC

1 Clara Malraux, *Nos Vingt Ans* (Paris: Grasset 1966), 56.

2 The interview, in three parts, was broadcast by the ORTF on Channel One on 2, 4, and 5 Oct. 1967.

3 Malraux, "Mobilités," *Action*, July 1920.

4 Malraux, *Royaume-farfelu* (Geneva: Skira 1945), 151.

5 Ibid., 131, 139; Malraux, "Journal d'un pompier du jeu de massacre," *Action*, Aug. 1921; Malraux, *Royaume-farfelu*, 139.

6 Malraux, "Journal d'un pompier du jeu de massacre," 26.

7 Malraux, "Les Hérissons apprivoisés," *Signaux de France et de Belgique*, 1 Aug. 1921.

8 Clara Malraux, *Les Combats et les jeux* (Paris: Grasset 1967), 13.

9 This text appears in an appendix to the French version of Walter Langlois' study of Malraux and Indochina: *L'Aventure indochinoise* (Paris: Mercure de France 1967), 323.

10 In Jean Lacouture, *André Malraux: Une vie dans le siècle* (Paris: Seuil 1973), 131.

11 Sigmund Freud, *Le Mot d'esprit et ses rapports avec l'inconscient* (Paris: Gallimard 1971), 355; Henri Bergson, *Le Rire: Essai sur la signification du comique* (Paris: Presses Universitaires de France 1956), 4.

12 Malraux, *Les Conquérants* (Paris: Grasset 1928), 14.

13 I return to the cat as an omnipresent element in Malraux's world in chapter 9.

14 Malraux, "Du livre," *Catalogue d'éditions originales et de livres illustrés*, no. 11 (Paris: Gallimard 1929).

15 It is worth recalling that throughout his life Malraux indulged a curious penchant for charmingly bizarre drawings of "dyables," ranging in subject from the quaintness of roller-skated birds to the disturbing portrayal of skewered chickens and flattened foxes!

16 Malraux, *Le Temps du mépris*, published in serial form in *La Nouvelle Revue française*, May 1935, 736.

17 Malraux, *L'Espoir*, 69.
18 Malraux, *La Condition humaine*, 210.
19 Ibid., 210.
20 Malraux, *Les Noyers de l'Altenburg*, 104–5.
21 Malraux, "Sur Goya," *Le Triangle noir* (Paris: Gallimard 1970), 75.
22 Malraux, *La Corde et les souris*, 178.
23 See Malraux, *Antimémoires*, 475, and *La Corde et les souris*, 179.
24 Malraux, *La Corde et les souris*, 179.
25 Ibid., 179.
26 Malraux, *Antimémoires*, 475.
27 Ibid., 477.
28 Ibid., 475.
29 Malraux, *La Corde et les souris*, 60.
30 Ibid., 441.
31 Ibid.
32 Malraux, *Antimémoires*, 65.
33 Malraux, *La Corde et les souris*, 464.
34 Ibid., 340.
35 Ibid., 396.
36 Malraux, *L'Homme précaire et la littérature* (Paris: Gallimard 1977), 308.
37 This information comes from the poet Pierre Béarn, an early friend of Malraux.
38 Malraux, *Antimémoires*, 464.
39 Malraux refers to this "sourire" on several occasions in *Les Voix du silence*.

ON TIBETAN SYMBOLISM

1 André Malraux, *Le Tentation de l'Occident* (Paris: Grasset 1964).
2 For example, Malraux made frequent references to Tibet and its capacity to teach us certain truths in a major speech delivered in Holland in 1930. A report of this event appears in *Mélanges Malraux* 8, no. 1 (1976), entitled "Les Expressions suprêmes de l'homme en Asie."
3 Malraux, *La Condition humaine*, 188.
4 Very occasionally they are discovered on *thankas* of the Red Dakini or Tara. Only one instance, reported by Gilles Béguin of the Musée Guimet, has come to light of a *thanka* where the skeletons are the principal figures. Photographs of that *thanka*, which is situated in a temple in Ladakh, have not yet been published.
5 See René de Nebesky-Wojkowitz, *Oracles and Demons of Tibet* (The Hague: Mouton 1956), 83.
6 See E. Pander, *Das Pantheon des Tschangtscha Hutuktu* (Berlin, n.p. 1980).
7 "Durkrod-bdagpo" in Tibetan; "Citipati" is the Sanskrit version more generally used by iconographers.

8 See Alice Getty, *The Gods of Northern Buddhism* (Oxford: Clarendon 1914), 153.

9 See L.A. Waddell, *The Buddhism of Tibet or Lamaism* (Cambridge: Heffer 1959), 525.

10 It would be wise at this point to insist that iconography is just like literary criticism in that, happily, it does not lend itself to any absolute and exhaustively correct exegesis. In this vein it is worth including, as a minor critical restraint, the unusual interpretation given by Eleanor Olson in her book, *Tantric Buddhist Art* (New York: China Institute 1974), of a late seventeenth-century bronze of the Citipati: "The happy pair, with legs interlaced, dance upon a sea of blood, holding in their left hands well-filled skull-cups. Their raised right hands hold peacock-feathers and a fish-tailed club with skull-top. The triangular form of the base is symbolic of the blazing fire of wisdom which consumes ignorance. The pair symbolize unity in duality and naked Reality stripped of all wordly illusions. They dance in joyous freedom" (30–1).

11 It may be of interest to point to Malraux's continuing fascination with skeletons. For example, the text of *Lunes en papier* features such a creature, as does the frontispiece for the first book Malraux designed for Kra – Rémy de Gourmont's *Le Livret de l'imagier*.

12 These terms place the accent on interdependence and unity rather than on dissimilarity.

13 Georges Bataille, *L'Erotisme* (Paris: Union Générale d'Editions 1975), 20.

14 Malraux, *Les Conquérants*, 138. See chapter 3 of this book also.

15 Malraux, *La Voie royale*, 10.

16 Malraux, *La Condition humaine*, 188.

17 Malraux, "Lawrence et l'érotisme," *La Nouvelle Revue française*, no. 220 (1932): 138.

18 Malraux, *La Condition humaine*, 85.

19 Malraux, "Lawrence et l'érotisme," 136.

ON THE RENUNCIATION
OF THE NOVEL

1 *Liberté de l'esprit* (Apr. 1949): 9.

2 Malraux, "Esquisse d'une psychologie du cinéma," *Scènes choisies* (Paris: Gallimard 1946), 331.

3 *French Studies* (July 1971); Jean Carduner, *La Création romanesque chez Malraux* (Paris: Nizet 1968).

4 In an unpublished conversation with Professor C.J. Greshoff in 1967.

5 See chapter 2.

6 Malraux, *Les Conquérants*, 128–9.

7 Ibid., 122–3.

8 G. Rees, "Animal Imagery in the Novels of André Malraux," *French Studies*

(Apr. 1955) confirms the comparative richness in this respect of *La Voie royale*.

9 Malraux, *La Voie royale*, 60, 73.

10 Ibid., 122, 127, 137, 142.

11 Ibid., 39.

12 Malraux, *La Condition humaine*, 7.

13 Claude-Edmonde Magny, *L'Age du roman américain* (Paris: Seuil 1945), 5.

14 Malraux, *La Condition humaine*, 7.

15 Cf. ibid., 10, 13, 14, 21, 149, 150, 243, 252.

16 Ibid., 30.

17 In his analysis of both *La Condition humaine* and *L'Espoir*, Carduner details several techniques of a cinematographic nature (e.g., travelling, fade-out, crossing-up, sound-track).

18 "C'est un navet" (according to Malraux) in Roger Stéphane, *Fin d'une jeunesse* (Paris: La Table Ronde 1954), 32.

19 R. Brasillach, "*La Condition humaine*," *Action française*, 10 Aug. 1933.

20 It is noticeable that the use of free indirect style in the subsequent novels is far more sparing.

21 Cf. Gaëtan Picon, *Malraux par lui-même* (Paris: Seuil 1970), 66.

22 Malraux, "Préface," in André Viollis, *Indochine S.O.S.* (Paris: Gallimard 1935), vii.

23 Cf. Malraux, *L'Espoir*. Only 47 pages out of a total of 487 (88–91, 228–35, 252–7, 271–3, 322–5, 326–32, 342–3, 396–8, 406–13, 474–5).

24 Malraux, *L'Espoir*, 349.

25 It was worth recalling that critic and film director Pier-Paolo Pasolini has often related his "cinéma de poésie" to free indirect style in literature.

26 See Carduner's conscientious analysis.

27 Malraux, *L'Espoir*, 31.

28 Ibid., 239.

29 See note 19 above.

30 See chapter 1.

ON "SIERRA DE TERUEL"

1 Published as a "document annexe" in André Bazin, *Le Cinéma de l'Occupation et de la Résistance* (Paris: Union Générale d'Editions 1975), 190.

2 In an interview with Michel Droit, *Le Figaro littéraire*, 23 Oct. 1967, 3.

3 Ibid., 7.

4 Cf. Malraux, *Scènes choisies*, 331.

5 Cf. Denis Marion, *André Malraux* (Paris: Seghers 1970); Franz J. Albersmeier, *André Malraux und der Film* (Bern/Frankfurt: Lang 1973); John Michalczyk, *André Malraux's "Espoir"* (St. Louis, Missouri: Missouri University Press 1977); Robert Thornberry, *André Malraux et l'Espagne* (Geneva: Droz 1977).

6 Malraux, *Scènes choisies*, 332.
7 See note 1 above.
8 Marcel Martin, *Le Langage cinématographique* (Paris: Cerf 1971), 169; Pierre Galante, *André Malraux* (Paris: Presses de la Cité 1970).
9 Quoted in Louis Aragon, "Reconnaissance à André Malraux," *Ce soir*, 12 Aug. 1939, 3.
10 E.g., R. Leenhardt, "André Malraux et le cinéma," *Fontaine* (1945): 403.
11 See note 1 above.
12 Bazin, *Le Cinéma de l'Occupation et de la Résistance*, 176.
13 R. Leavitt, "Music in the Aesthetics of André Malraux," *French Review* (Oct. 1956): 25–30.
14 André Malraux, *Le Temps du mépris*, in *La Nouvelle Revue française* (Apr. 1935): 410.
15 Ibid.

ON FELINE FORMS

1 Charles Baudelaire, *Les Fleurs du mal* (Paris: Garnier 1961), 56.
2 Malraux, "Mobilités," *Action*, July 1920.
3 Malraux, *Lunes en papier*, 160–1.
4 Ibid., 163.
5 Ibid.
6 See chapter 5.
7 See Clara Malraux, *Les Combats et les jeux* (Paris: Grasset 1967), 13.
8 Malraux, *La Corde et les souris*, 446.
9 Malraux, "Du livre," introduction to *Catalogue d'éditions originales et de livres illustrés*, no. 11 (Paris: Gallimard 1929).
10 Malraux, *La Condition humaine,* 28.
11 Malraux, *L'Espoir*, 182.
12 Ibid., 273.
13 Malraux, *La Condition humaine*, 97.
14 Malraux, *La Corde et les souris*, 264; *Antimémoires*, 464.
15 Malraux, *La Corde et les souris*, 67.
16 Ibid., 201.
17 Lewis Carroll, *Alice in Wonderland* (New York: Bramhall House 1967), 87.
18 Ibid., 88.
19 Ibid., 89, 91, 116.
20 Malraux, *La Corde et les souris*, 624.
21 Malraux, *L'Homme précaire et la littérature*, 308.

ON DEATH AND DYING

1 Published in *Spécial* (Brussels), 30 Oct. 1974.
2 Roger Garaudy, "The Death Mask of André Malraux," *Literature of the*

Graveyard, trans. J.M. Bernstein (New York: International Publishers 1948), 24–49.

3 Serge Gaulupeau, *André Malraux et la mort* (Paris: Minard 1969), 53.

4 Thomas Jefferson Kline, *André Malraux and the Metamorphosis of Death* (New York: Columbia University Press 1973).

5 G.T. Harris, "Note on *Le Miroir des limbes:* A Convoy of Utopias and Aspirations," *Mélanges Malraux* 13, no. 2 (1981): 22–5.

6 Malraux, *Le Miroir des limbes* (Paris: Gallimard 1976), 179, 634.

7 Ibid., 873.

8 "Malraux parle," *Le Figaro littéraire*, 9 Oct. 1967, 14.

9 Malraux, "Mobilités," *Action*, July 1920.

10 Malraux, *Lunes en papier*, 186.

11 Malraux, *Les Conquérants*, 195.

12 Ibid., 283.

13 Malraux, *La Voie royale*, 176.

14 Ibid., 180, 181.

15 Malraux, *Le Miroir des limbes*, 276.

16 The manuscript of *La Voie royale* is in the Library of the University of Wyoming.

17 Malraux, *La Condition humaine*, 10.

18 Ibid., 190.

19 Ibid., 191.

20 Ibid.

21 Ibid., 246.

22 Ibid., 247.

23 Ibid., 246, 247.

24 Ibid., 252.

25 Malraux, *L'Espoir*, 252.

26 Ibid., 255.

27 Ibid., 253–4.

28 Ibid., 162.

29 Cited in Denis Marion, *André Malraux* (Paris: Seghers 1970), 102.

30 Malraux, *Les Noyers de l'Altenburg*, 90.

31 E.g., *L'Espoir*, 69, 273.

32 Malraux, *Les Noyers de l'Altenburg*, 91.

33 Malraux, *Le Miroir des limbes*, 837.

34 Ibid., 932.

35 Ibid.

36 Malraux, *Les Conquérants*, 216.

ON ORATORY

1 E.g., Jacqueline Leiner, "Autour d'un discours de Malraux," *Série Malraux* I (1972): 47–59: "une étude approfondie du texte [du discours

"L'Art est une conquête"] révèle l'existence d'un plan rigoureux et logique, une connaissance de l'art oratoire" (51).

2 Lacouture, *André Malraux: Une vie dans le siècle* (Paris: Seuil 1973), 67.

3 Ibid., 131.

4 François Mauriac, *Journal 1932–9* (Paris: La Table Ronde 1947), 293–4.

5 Reported in *Commune*, Sept. 1937, 41–3.

6 Claude Mauriac, *Un autre de Gaulle: Journal 1944–54* (Paris: Hachette 1970), 313.

7 Malraux, "Préface," *Oraisons funèbres* (Paris: Gallimard 1971), 9–12.

8 Malraux, *Les Conquérants*, 153.

9 Malraux, *La Condition humaine*, 113.

10 Malraux, *Antimémoires*, 336.

11 Malraux, *La Corde et les souris*, 23.

12 Malraux, *Antimémoires*, 171.

13 Brigitte Friang, *Un autre Malraux* (Paris: Plon 1977), 90.

14 See Julien Green, *Journal*, I, 1928–39 (Paris: Plon 1954), 26.

15 W.H. Frohock, "Malraux: The Tragic Sensibility," *Dalhousie French Studies* 2 (Oct. 1980): 89–100.

16 Malraux, *La Corde et les souris*, 41.

17 William Righter, *The Rhetorical Hero* (London: Routledge & Kegan Paul 1964), 30–1.

18 In reply to Gide's observation that there were only intellectuals in Malraux's novels.

19 Etienne Fuzellier, *Cinéma et littérature* (Paris: Du Cerf 1964), 49.

20 Such a division would respect *grosso modo* the spirit of the preface to the *Oraisons funèbres*.

21 Malraux, *Les Conquérants*, 49.

22 Ibid., 99.

23 It might be recalled that Gandhi, too, was recognized for his awareness of the value of an *object*: "Pour former l'avenir Gandhi faisait appel à des sentiments très anciens. Et puis il y avait son génie des symboles: le rouet, le sel. Ce qu'il proclamait surprenait par son évidence." Malraux, *Antimémoires*, 335.

24 Malraux, *Les Noyers de l'Altenburg*, 48.

25 For the purpose of this book extensive use was made of the record *André Malraux – discours historiques*, presented by Michel Cazenave, produced by the Institut Charles de Gaulle (Disques Déesse DDLX 83–4). Additional material was examined from the record *André Malraux – discours politiques*, presented by Pierre Durand in the series "Hommes et Faits du XXᵉ siècle" (Disques Serp). Apart from the *Oraisons funèbres* the best published collection of Malraux speech material is in *Espoir* (Revue de l'Institut Charles de Gaulle), no. 2 (Jan. 1973).

26 Ibid.

27 It would also be appropriate to acknowledge a *loss* of power late in his life, exacerbated by certain difficulties with breath control and articulation. There resulted on occasion a painfully fractured stutter instead of an intended rending cry.

28 Lacouture, *André Malraux: Une vie dans le siècle*, 312.

29 Ibid., 313.

30 Ibid., 337.

31 See note 25 above.

32 Ibid. The same evocation also occurs earlier, in his 2 July 1947 speech at the Vélodrome d'Hiver in Paris.

33 Cf. in particular Malraux's speech at the Plateau des Glières (Haute-Savoie) on 2 Sept. 1973 on the occasion of the "Inauguration du Monument à la mémoire des martyrs de la Résistance" published in *Le Miroir des limbes* (Paris: Gallimard 1976), 998–1005.

34 Malraux, *Oraisons funèbres*, 43.

35 Malraux, *Le Miroir des limbes*, 1000.

36 Malraux, *Oraisons funèbres*, 90–1.

37 Cf. *Oraisons funèbres*, 117–37 and the recording (note 25).

38 Of special interest, perhaps, is Malraux's return, on several occasions, to certain highly evocative passages because they communicated effectively the climate of the moment. Thus, for example, the following passage, which appears originally in the 1958 speech commemorating the liberation of Paris, is inserted impromptu into the "Glières" speech during delivery, and also recurs in the 1975 speech on the anniversary of the "Libération des camps de déportation": "Alors dans tous les bagnes depuis la Forêt-Noire jusqu'à la Baltique, l'immense cortège des ombres qui survivaient encore se leva sur ses jambes flageolantes. Et le peuple de ceux dont la technique concentrationnaire avait tenté de faire des esclaves parce qu'ils avaient été parfois des héros, pas encore délivré, encore en face de la mort, ressentit que même s'il ne devait jamais revoir la France, il mourrait avec une âme de vainqueur." (*Oraisons funèbres*, 29–30)

39 Examples of the above are to be found throughout the "Glières" and "Jean Moulin" speeches. In addition, a particularly significant occurrence can be pointed to on the occasion of Malraux's decisive speech to the MLN in Jan. 1945. The insistent repetition of "nous" and its derivatives serves to evoke an exclusive solidarity among the Resistance members that makes the idea of fusion with the Communist party or any other group unthinkable:

A cette époque *nous* avons eu en face de *nous* une armée puissante. *Nous* avons aussi été beaucoup aidés. Lorsque *nous* avons vu arriver tous ceux des *nôtres* qui avaient pu rejoindre l'Algérie et *nous* avons vu arriver enfin l'armée des grands empires, l'armée bien équipée: *nous* étions la France en haillons; mais c'est elle qui a permis à l'armée qui débarquait d'arriver à temps à Paris ...

Messieurs, la situation dans laquelle *nous nous* trouvons est exactement celle de cette époque-là ... *Nous* ne sommes pas une association d'anciens combattants qui viennent demander à qui que ce soit une aide, une reconnaissance ou des places au nom de leurs vieilles médailles. *Nous* sommes des combattants encore vivants qui seront capables de refaire demain ce qu'ils ont fait hier." *Premier Congrès National: Mouvement de libération nationale* (Sceaux: MLN 1945), 1304, my emphasis.

40 Malraux, *Oraisons funèbres*, 114.
41 Malraux, *Le Temps du mépris*, serialized in *La Nouvelle Revue française* (1935), 733.
42 Malraux, *Antimémoires*, 195.
43 See note 25 above.
44 Friang, *Un autre Malraux*, 140.
45 Ibid., 142.
46 Malraux, *Oraisons funèbres*, 10.
47 Quoted by Pol Gaillard, *Malraux* (Paris: Bordas 1970), 99.
48 Malraux, *Antimémoires*, 163.
49 Ibid., 165.
50 See note 25 above.
51 Lacouture, *André Malraux: Une vie dans le siècle*, 381.
52 See note 25 above.
53 Malraux, *Le Temps du mépris*, 735.

CONCLUSION

1 Malraux, *L'Homme précaire et la littérature*, 8, 199.
2 Cathleen Healey, "Entretien avec André Malraux," *Mélanges Malraux* 12, no. 1: 20.
3 Ibid., 21.
4 Malraux, *L'Homme précaire et la littérature*, 329, 330–1.
5 Malraux, "D'une jeunesse européenne," *Ecrits* (Paris: Grasset 1927), 152, 153.
6 Malraux, "Préface" to Manès Sperber, *Qu'une larme dans l'océan* (Paris: Calmann-Lévy 1952).
7 Healey, "Entretien avec André Malraux," 22.

Index